Traumatized Church worked like a meat tenderizer on the hard, self-reliant lumps in my heart that seem to form overnight when I'm not vigilant about guarding it. McKnight and Gibson's compelling and complex portrait of the agony and angst Paul went through when he was dealing with the Corinthian church is a poignant reminder that perfection is not a prerequisite for spiritual efficacy. The fact that at least one chapter in this great apostle's story reveals tearstains on his face and grooves of grief in his soul proves we don't have to curate our emotions to effectively communicate the unconditional love of Jesus Christ. And isn't it almost always an acute awareness of our own brokenness that gives birth to the humility necessary for deep healing? Blessed are the vulnerable, because their longing for reconciliation points us all to the only true healer.

—Lisa Harper, bestselling author, sought-after Bible teacher, and host of the *Back Porch Theology podcast*

Every pastor I know will find themselves nodding their heads as they read *Traumatized Church.* Laypeople, too, will recognize how trauma has shaped their congregations. Though I've studied Paul for a lifetime, McKnight and Gibson have changed how I will see Paul and read 2 Corinthians. This is such a great book! If you've known pain in your church or in your ministry, or if you've struggled with Paul, you will find this book a remarkable gift.

—Adam Hamilton, Senior Pastor, The United Methodist Church of the Resurrection; author, *The Call: The Life and Message of the Apostle Paul*

In *Traumatized Church,* we meet St. Paul as we've never seen him: as a traumatized apostle. McKnight, a leading New Testament scholar, and Gibson, an experienced counselor, offer compelling stories and accessible information about the nature of trauma and how we can heal from it. Their persuasive arguments empower churches to establish and maintain healthy cultures and trauma-sensitive spaces. Scripture, read through a trauma lens, comes alive with hope and healing as the gospel reshapes our trauma through reflection on Christ's life.

—Lynn Cohick, Distinguished Professor of New Testament, Houston Christian University

Traumatized Church gives us permission to see Paul as the weary and wounded human being he was: a gifted leader with a battered nervous system attempting to cope in his ministry context. It reminds us that holiness has never required superhuman strength—only honesty, humility, and hope.

—Dr. Chuck DeGroat, Founding Executive Director, Clinical Mental Health Counseling Program, Western Theological Seminary; author, *When Narcissism Comes to Church*

This book offers a compassionate, wise, and much needed guide for those who long for churches to become safer places for the wounded in a season marked by culture wars, pastoral abuse scandals, and corrupted leadership models within the American evangelical church. With deep biblical grounding and trauma-informed insight, McKnight and Gibson teach us how to listen well, tell the truth with care, and embody Christ's healing presence in communities that desperately need restoration.

—Rev. Caleb E. Campbell, author, *Disarming Leviathan: Loving Your Christian Nationalist Neighbor*

In *Traumatized Church*, McKnight and Gibson provide a fresh look at the significance of human experience in how we perceive God and participate in our Christian communities, even when that experience is traumatizing. But we aren't alone. Through the lens of the apostle Paul and his own experiences with trauma, McKnight and Gibson offer a safe space for Christians to journey toward hope and healing, to become trauma healthy. This book is a gift to the church as it reveals how we can heal from our trauma. But *Traumatized Church* also offers the necessary preventive steps so that the church might be the safe place it was always intended to be.

—Dr. Kyle DiRoberts, Chair and Associate Professor of Biblical and Theological Studies, Arizona Christian University; author, *The Secret to Prayer* and *Grace Beyond Salvation*

Gibson and McKnight have composed literary balm for those souls carrying the burden of trauma or who have acquired trauma from their own churches. They explain how the apostle Paul experienced trauma, and map his response to it in 2 Corinthians. Using first-person stories, Gibson and McKnight provide some advice on trauma recovery, on creating trauma-aware churches, and on how to move from trauma to healing and hope.

—Rev. Dr. Michael F. Bird (PhD, University of Queensland), Deputy Principal, Ridley College, Melbourne, Australia

Paul failed to measure up to the expectations of his converts in Corinth. That put the apostle in a tough spot, having to defend himself to the very people who benefited from his ministry—a challenge many ministers know all too well. We may identify with Paul's plight. But according to McKnight and Gibson, we should also find great wisdom in how he responded to his naysayers. Whether we're professional ministers or amateurs like Paul, *Traumatized Church* is a timely word that helps us face and overcome a timeless problem: healing for Christians wounded by Christians.

—Rodney Reeves, Senior Pastor, First Baptist Church, Jonesboro, Arkansas

How does reading Paul as one who experienced trauma change how we view the apostle? In *Traumatized Church*, McKnight and Gibson depict a vulnerable Paul whose pain and trauma both shape his relationship with the Corinthians and offer insights into how the church today may respond to the needs of its leaders and laity who are experiencing trauma. This book is a provocative analysis of trauma theory applied to Paul's Corinthian correspondence. While one may not agree with all of the claims or interpretive trajectories in this study, it raises important and necessary questions regarding the church, pastoral leadership, relationship between congregants, and abuse in congregations. This book deserves a careful read by anyone interested in the contemporary applicability of the Pauline epistles.

—Lisa Bowens, Associate Professor of New Testament, Princeton Theological Seminary

How might having a trauma therapist reading over the shoulder of a biblical scholar help us to read Paul's correspondence with the Corinthians afresh? This new look at 2 Corinthians humanizes Paul as an apostle traumatized by the verbal abuse he received from some Corinthian Christ-followers. McKnight and Gibson weave a close reading of 2 Corinthians with compelling stories that illustrate how unhealthy power dynamics and misbehavior have scarred pastors and congregants. Presented here is a vision for how a trauma-informed church might nurture healthy boundaries, mutuality, and the empowerment of its members, while also safeguarding itself against abuse. Reading about Paul's emotions and his strained relationship with the Corinthians invites readers to reflect on their emotional lives and critically consider the power dynamics operating in their churches through a trauma-informed lens.

—T. Christopher Hoklotubbe, Associate Professor of Indigenous Theological Studies at the Indigenous Theological Circle at Bexley Seabury Seminary; Director of Graduate Studies at NAIITS: An Indigenous Learning Community

Traumatized Church

Traumatized Church

What Paul's Relationship with the Corinthian Church Teaches Us About Helping Those Who Are Hurting

SCOT McKNIGHT AND
ADRIENNE GIBSON

ZONDERVAN REFLECTIVE

Traumatized Church

Published by Zondervan, 3950 Sparks Drive SE, Suite 101, Grand Rapids, MI 49546, USA. Zondervan is a registered trademark of The Zondervan Corporation, L.L.C., a wholly owned subsidiary of HarperCollins Christian Publishing, Inc.

Requests for information should be addressed to customercare@harpercollins.com.

Zondervan titles may be purchased in bulk for educational, business, fundraising, or sales promotional use. For information, please email SpecialMarkets@Zondervan.com.

ISBN 978-0-310-17980-1 (softcover)
ISBN 978-0-310-17982-5 (audio)
ISBN 978-0-310-17981-8 (ebook)

HarperCollins Publishers, Macken House, 39/40 Mayor Street Upper, Dublin 1, D01 C9W8, Ireland (https://www.harpercollins.com)

Cover design: Thinkpen Design
Cover photo and art: © Adri / Adobe Stock
Interior design: Kristina Juodenas

Printed in the United States of America

26 27 28 29 30 LBC 5 4 3 2 1

Scot and Kris

For Kelly and Karen

Adrienne

To my safe and secure spot, the place I call home.
Wherever the four of you are,
that's where I want to be:
Matthew, Ryland, London, and Anneliese

Contents

Part 4: Trauma Healthy: The Whole Body

Preface

People at times need protection from pastors, and pastors at times need protection from people because, well, people need protection from people. People hurt people. Sometimes intentionally, sometimes unintentionally. Churches and Christian institutions are not always safe spaces. This book aims to help them become safe spaces.

Our book integrates two dimensions of Christianity: trauma therapy and the apostle Paul's seemingly over-the-top responses to accusations against him. Trauma studies informs us about Paul, and Paul informs us about trauma.

The book has four parts: "Trauma Informed," "Trauma Sensitive," "Trauma Safe," and "Trauma Healthy." The first and third are informed by trauma therapy, and the second is a more extensive look at Paul in light of the first. The implications of integrating the first and second parts are spelled out in the third part, and the final part offers practical suggestions for Christian organizations that strive to become trauma healthy.

In one sense, this book is for those who want to understand a perplexing Paul as revealed in a perplexing section of one of his letters. In another sense, this book is for Christian organizations that want to become trauma informed, trauma sensitive, trauma safe, and trauma healthy by showing how these important themes are found already in the New Testament. In yet another sense, this book is for churches that see church people who are in the trauma zone and want to know how they can nurture a culture that is trauma safe for the wounded. One more "in another sense": We know that trauma-safe spaces will be nurtured in Christian spaces only when leaders (pastors, administrators, directors, presidents) commit to become trauma informed, and then commit leadership to implement the principles needed to create trauma-safe spaces. So we pray that such leaders will read this book and absorb and implement its ideas.

We, Adrienne Gibson, a trauma therapist, and Scot McKnight, a New Testament professor, wrote this book together. Adrienne commented on what Scot wrote, and Scot commented on what Adrienne wrote. The genesis of this book was Adrienne's master's thesis in her New Testament program in seminary. Scot was her supervisor. While reading her thesis, Scot more than once mentioned to his wife, Kris, who is a therapist, that Adrienne's thesis needed to be turned into a book somehow. So we ended up writing this book together. Adrienne wrote the trauma stuff, and Scot wrote the Paul stuff.

Adrienne's central ideas reshaped Scot's reading of the apostle Paul's second letter to the Corinthians, especially the last four chapters. Adrienne's trauma-informed ideas gave Scot ears to hear what Paul was writing that he had never heard before. So we will begin with discussions of what trauma is and what it does before we get to Paul. Only in understanding trauma theory can we resonate with Paul's experiences. Our discussion of trauma provides crucial insights into the condition of this man who was far more vulnerable and in pain than many people today recognize. After we have shed light on trauma, on Paul, and on how trauma studies enable us to understand Paul more insightfully, we will turn to practices that Christian individuals and institutions can embrace to create trauma-healthy spaces.

The whole body is needed for a place to become trauma healthy.

The mind needs to be trauma informed, the ears need to become trauma sensitive, and the eyes need to look for what is trauma safe as the whole body yearns for spaces that are trauma healthy.

PART 1

Trauma Informed

THE MIND

Chapter 1

Understanding Trauma: A Sketch

Judith Herman wrote *the* book on trauma, in which she describes what trauma does to a person: "Traumatic events overwhelm the ordinary systems of care that give people a sense of control, connection and meaning."[1] Trauma, at its basic level, is an event or an experience that overwhelms our capacity to cope.[2] We begin to understand trauma, which is best diagnosed by a therapist, by starting with three terms: a *response* to an event, an experience, or a culture that *overwhelms* and *affects* and even threatens a person's identity, security, and safety.

Because trauma is complex, we can expound on what it is a little more. The Substance Abuse and Mental Health Services Administration (SAMHSA) expands these three terms (response, overwhelms, affects) as follows: Trauma "results from an event, series of events, or set of circumstances that is experienced by an individual as physically or emotionally harmful or life threatening and that has lasting effects on the person's functioning and mental, physical, social, emotional, or spiritual well-being."[3]

Trauma describes the feelings and states of being overwhelmed.

Peter Levine, an expert on healing trauma, has concluded that "we become traumatized when our ability to respond to a perceived threat is in some way overwhelmed. This inability to adequately respond can impact us in obvious ways, as well as ways that are subtle."[4] Being overwhelmed describes the entire person. Bessel van der Kolk, a Dutch psychiatrist who is known for his pioneering work on the impact of trauma on the whole body, defines trauma as follows: "Trauma is not just an event that took place sometime in the past; it is also the imprint left by that experience on mind, brain, and body. . . . Trauma results in a fundamental reorganization of the way the mind and brain manage perceptions. It changes not only how we think and what we think about, but also our very capacity to think."[5] For van der Kolk, events or a series of events that are physically or emotionally harmful precipitate trauma in a person. Those who are working with wounded folks need to recognize both the subjective and the perceptive nature of trauma. People feel it. They may not at first even know that what they are experiencing is trauma. Over time, however, those in the trauma zone know they are in it. They perceive it themselves.

Two more terms help us understand trauma's pervasive and subtle impacts. They are *memory* and *intention*. Trauma forms a memory. The word often used, *trigger*, points to a person's embodied memory. The traumatized person's body remembers the event or experience, and that person relives the event as if it were occurring in the present. Here's an example. Nancy French, a *New York Times* bestselling author and investigative journalist, on her Twitter account (now called "X"), announced to her friends, one of whom is my (Scot) wife, Kris, that she was about to begin the "red devil" chemo for her cancer treatment. "Side effects are serious—If I cry, it'll be red tears!—so please pray."[6] Samuel Perry (@profsamperry), a professor in Oklahoma, responded to Nancy French with words that illustrate the memory at work in traumatized persons. "Stay strong, Nancy. We've been there. I'd say my wife could go on and on about the 'red devil' Adriamycin, but she can't without wanting to vomit. Doesn't even like the sight of red liquid (e.g., Kool-Aid, cough medicine)." Sam Perry's wife's body remembers her physical trauma. Trauma is a memory. Trauma's memory is God's design to protect us.

Thus, a person experiences something—sexual abuse, verbal abuse, emotional abuse, COVID-19, the death of a parent, child, spouse, sibling, or friend, a murder or a horrendous crash—and that experience overwhelms them. The experiences of being overwhelmed include anxiety, depression, fear, and even dissociation.

A female pastor a few summers ago helped lead a mission trip to Latvia. This was her fourth summer taking this trip and working with the same organization. She was joined by her husband and two teenage sons. Her eldest son has bipolar disorder and experienced a manic episode while in Latvia. Both this woman and her husband rushed to take care of their son. Unfortunately, they were both later reprimanded by leaders back at their home church for not making the other students their focus in the aftercare because the episode was witnessed by most of the students on the trip. To be clear, this mom and dad were not the only leaders on this trip. There were at least six other adults from the home church responsible for the care of the other high school students.

The meetings held to discuss the event after their return to the United States created their trauma. They were asked to relive that moment over and over again and to answer questions as to why they did what they did and why they did not do what they did not do. They were asked why they responded the way they did. The mother was reminded, over and over again, that she was, at the moment of her son's manic episode, physically separated from her son. Over and over again, she had to recall his being without her. While dealing with the guilt this brought, she was also told she had handled the situation poorly and had not done enough for the rest of the team. The meetings and interrogations that followed asked for detailed explanations, which tore at her and beat her up further. She was led to believe she had made a huge mistake, that she had done everything wrong. While craving empathy and compassion, she was met with criticism and correction. The meetings, emails, and corrections took place for six months, during which the family felt attacked and not cared for. They needed love and support and healing. Eventually, she resigned and the family left the church, where they had been for more than twenty-five years. The anxiety of that never-ending narrative finally had become too much for her and her husband.

In this situation we see the negative result of a church community's lack of a trauma-informed understanding. The church's response led to paralyzing anxiety for this woman. She found herself not wanting to go to work and do the things she had once looked forward to doing. She felt a tight band around her head that frequently led to headaches. She found it hard to be around other people and to trust them as she once had—perhaps rightfully so. On top of that, she struggled with being able to trust herself at work or when around people from work. Her eyes and face would twitch. The repeated questions at the meetings and interrogations made her question everything. Her feet felt electrified, like she needed to get up and run away from it all. Anxiety paralyzed her ability to make decisions, and she experienced dread in places and situations where she wouldn't normally. Anxiety is our struggle to make sense of things that once made sense and no longer do. Her trauma was not heard or understood. It was not met with a soft heart or with words of compassion and empathetic witness. So she continued in a trauma-survival narrative, pushed on by incessant questions, while her inner world was fired up with anxiety.

Recently I learned of a young woman whose dissociation resulted from being traumatized by her father. The Mayo Clinic helps us better understand the term *dissociation*.

> Dissociative disorders are mental health conditions that involve experiencing a loss of connection between thoughts, memories, feelings, surroundings, behavior and identity. These conditions include escape from reality in ways that are not wanted and not healthy. This causes problems in managing everyday life.
>
> Dissociative disorders usually arise as a reaction to shocking, distressing or painful events and help push away difficult memories. Symptoms depend in part on the type of dissociative disorder and can range from memory loss to disconnected identities. Times of stress can worsen symptoms for a while, making them easier to see. . . .
>
> Symptoms depend on the type of dissociative disorder, but may include:
>
> - A sense of being separated from yourself and your emotions.
> - Thinking that people and things around you are distorted and not real.
> - A blurred sense of your own identity.
> - Severe stress or problems in relationships, work or other important areas of life.
> - Not being able to cope well with emotional or work-related stress.
> - Memory loss, also called amnesia, of certain time periods, events, people and personal information.
> - Mental health problems, such as depression, anxiety, and suicidal thoughts and behaviors.[7]

This young woman had been dissociating for several years, had found a therapist to be helpful, and was making slow but genuine progress in coming to terms with trauma. Dissociation is a more severe response to trauma, but it can serve as an example of what happens when a person is overwhelmed by an experience or event.

The singular, instinctual response to being overwhelmed is

protection, which is how God created us to be safe. Yet the body's response of trauma can be perceptive. That is, a person can perceive a threat, whether or not it is a real threat, as we saw in the example of Samuel Perry's wife earlier. Once a person has been traumatized by an event or an experience, a memory lodges deep in their heart, reminding the person to protect herself.

America's major cities, including Chicago, where Scot lives, have a crime problem. The constant news about Chicago's crime produces clicks and views and ads. As a result, we (Scot and Kris) get lots of news about all the crime in Chicago—carjackings, murders, thefts, break-ins, rapes, and abductions. After reading and hearing all this discouraging news, if a woman was suddenly to find herself dropped off at a (perceived or not) wrong stop on the train or bus, her body might enter a state of (perceived) fear for her safety. Upon arriving safely where she needs to go, she may even realize she has experienced trauma. And if she previously has been robbed or held at gunpoint in a similar location, her body might immediately respond as if it were under threat simply by finding herself in a perceived dangerous location.

This is not just a theory or what-if situation. Trauma embeds itself deeply in our memories. People are sitting in churches with embodied memories of trauma. Words in sermons, names mentioned, or even suddenly seeing someone who looks like a person who abused them might trigger a person's memory, and trauma can occur, right then and there. As much as 40 percent of a congregation has trauma stored in their memories. Awareness of this reality can help to transform a church culture for those who have been traumatized, and nonawareness of this can (unintentionally) retraumatize those who are under our care.

Let's take a look at another helpful term, *intention*, which is really a duality of terms. Experts in trauma do not focus on the intention of the person whose behaviors created trauma in a person. They concentrate instead on the impact of those behaviors. Whether intended or not, the person responsible for the behaviors is a factor in the trauma. So trauma is shaped not by a person's intention but by the impact of a person or an experience. For example, Scot's wife, Kris, was recently reading a book about a young woman who was pursuing ordination. Her denominationally appointed mentor occasionally transgressed lines in ways that made the young woman uncomfortable, even if her discomfort was hidden below the surface. That discomfort worked its way into this young woman's body and ended up becoming a serious case of trauma. When she reported her situation, an in-house (rather than an independent) investigation occurred. A striking result of the investigation was that they did not discover any bad intentions in the mentor. Had that investigation been trauma informed, the investigation would have focused not on the mentor's intention but on the impact of the mentor's actions on the young woman. The impact was more than obvious, because the woman's trauma had led her physician to question whether she might have a serious disease. This example illustrates why, when diagnosing trauma, we need to distinguish the oft-claimed intention of the one whose actions have wounded a person from the impact those actions have on them.

A friend who is also a pastor, whom I (Scot) know to be humble and teachable, shared his story of abuse and trauma with me. It began with a longtime member of the church, whom we will call Mateo. Like most congregants, Mateo was initially supportive of the pastor, though it didn't take long before he was expressing disagreement and creating disruption. I have edited parts of this story with the pastor's approval.

> Mateo began asking more and more questions at Sunday school and Bible studies. He didn't agree with how or what I taught. . . . He questioned me at church in the mornings, at Bible studies, and even in emails. He also started questioning my wife. Mateo stopped greeting me at church and even stopped shaking my hand, stating

quite loudly in front of others that he didn't want to shake my hand. (Handshaking was a cultural expression of fellowship in our church.) His questions turned into challenges, followed by Mateo going to the others and telling them not to listen to me and that he would teach them the truth. The challenges turned into yelling at me, shouting in disagreement.

This came to a head one night when I told him to stop. He didn't. Members of the congregation who had witnessed his behavior told him to stop. Several people complained to the board, and an emergency board meeting was held. The entire church came out to see what would be done.

But, out of the blue, the board members proceeded to question me. To my surprise, I was now on trial for mistreating Mateo. When I told the story of what was happening, the church members, who were once vocally against Mateo's bad behavior, were dead quiet. The board portrayed Mateo as merely a Berean seeking the truth. I was shocked and confused. I felt abandoned. So I described the story of Mateo's actions—about the lessons and his reactions, about his divisive comments, and about his slanderous accusations, calling me a false teacher. (I also explained what a Berean was from Acts 17, but this didn't persuade the board.) Silence. The board dismissed the meeting, agreeing to investigate and revisit the subject.

Another board meeting occurred the next day, but this one was a private meeting. The board had scheduled a meeting with just me. I was on trial for my behavior. Defending myself was taken by them as unbecoming of a pastor and clearly meant that I had anger issues. They questioned my call and if I was sure that God called me to be a pastor. I asked where I acted unbecoming and where I spoke in anger. I was told my response concerning Mateo and his lack of Berean-like humility was the angriest they had ever seen anyone. The board told me they had never seen a pastor act like that. I found

> this odd and was confused as witnesses (two separate families, eight people in all) of that previous night had actually approached me to ask how I stayed so calm and collected and how I recalled all of the events while staying composed. I responded by telling the board that I had never seen a Christian act like I had seen Mateo act, nor had I seen so many people defend such poor behavior. Two of the members of the board were people who had told Mateo he was out of line at the Bible studies. Now they were silent.

Earlier, we said that trauma is complex and complicated, and stories like this one reveal why. Many stories of trauma are the result of ongoing interactions and accusations and frustrations and insinuations. Many of us lack the wisdom to say the right thing in the right moment in the middle of a rancorous, disruptive meeting. Doing the right thing at the right time requires wisdom and experience. Most of us don't have sufficient experience with trauma, so we go silent. In this example, the voices that mattered for this pastor, those that would affirm his story, capitulated to a disruptive person, and it ended up deeply wounding the pastor. He closed this section of his story with these sentences: "I don't want to hold grudges and am trying to live out Jesus' call to forgive and love our enemies. Writing this has been difficult." I know this pastor. He loves God, he loves God's Word, he loves pastoring, and he loves God's people. But he has been wounded by an abusive congregant, one who was not confronted or challenged by church leaders who failed to do the right thing.

Chapter 2

Trauma: More Than an Event

A traumatic event leaves behind the calling card of trauma, but trauma is far more than the event or experience itself. Trauma is more than a doctor's message of a life-threatening disease. The message is the event, and trauma is the body's response to that event. Trauma is perception, and that is why many accurately say trauma is subjective. Trauma is about our personal (perceived or not perceived) response and its impact in our bodies and on our whole lives. For our purposes, these three words—perception, subjective, personal—overlap with one another. Taken together they summarize the impact of a traumatizing event on someone's inner world.

Because we all have our own perceptions of who we are and what we can handle, trauma becomes bigger than the event itself because trauma is about living with the event and its ongoing impact on us. Trauma describes ongoing, recurring attempts to suppress or hide experiences of an event. The supports (or lack of support) we have to help us manage and heal our trauma also shape how we experience our trauma.

How we respond to trauma tends to fit well-known patterns. The experience or event is encoded into our bodies' memory as trauma when it becomes overwhelming. When this happens our bodies instinctually enter a mode called "survival." Again, it is good to remember that trauma is the body's *response* to the experience or event. Our bodies want peace and joy and trust—our bodies want safety—so they seek, chase, and fight for safety. Survival is about pursuing our own safety so we can live in peace with ourselves. When faced with a situation requiring survival, our bodies respond with several God-given techniques that help us pursue safety: fight, flight, freeze, fawn.

We'll go into more detail on each of these later. For now, the important thing for us to recognize is that these responses to trauma occur as we step into the emotional and physical storm of survival. We are not the same people when we are terrified and fighting for our lives as we are when we're calm and attuned and feeling at peace. Our bodies change in remarkable ways.

Some years ago I (Scot) served for a summer in a foreign country in a small ministry situation with a team of leaders. One of the members of the team was a rather large, loud man. I was young and unskilled and not able to perceive much that was going on behind closed doors. This man's wife rarely made eye contact. She had an unusual (at least in my experience) mousy voice. She spoke with all of us in everyday conversation with a higher than normal pitch. What was confusing was that whenever she sang solos or sang with others, a beautiful, melodious, deep, and powerful voice emerged. Years after this trip, we learned that her husband was severely abusive of her, both verbally and sexually, and sometime later she divorced him. Looking back on those days, I now recognize that her body's voice was a form of protection as she lived a traumatized existence. Her voice was a response of freezing, and her entire behavior was shaped by fawning to her abusive husband. I must add, too, that one or two times her husband was the Sunday preacher at the church, and he exhibited the least impressive talks I had ever heard. His sermons had neither depth nor spiritual perception. At the time, that was perhaps the only clue I recognized.

In this book we will be looking at someone who is almost never (and that's an understatement) brought into discussions of trauma. But if you look carefully at these four responses to trauma and then read how the apostle Paul responded to various factional leaders and congregations in Corinth, it is possible to map those responses onto Paul. I (Scot) am not the first to "diagnose" Paul with PTSD (post-traumatic stress disorder), or something akin to our modern diagnosis. Here's all one needs to do. Examine the four techniques we use to cope with the stresses of trauma and compare them with how Paul responds, and it becomes clear that his nastiness and defensiveness and avoidance all fit the diagnosis. The Corinthians beat Paul up, and he was overwhelmed. They were, not to put too a fine point on it, underwhelmed by him and his so-called giftedness.

At this point, some of you may have difficulty understanding why we are using Paul as an example of someone experiencing trauma. You might be muttering to yourself, *That man has traumatized me with his writings!* We understand why you feel that way. Many do. We do too, at times. We will explain why Paul has formed for us—a trauma therapist and a New Testament scholar—a surprising example of someone who was himself traumatized by Christians. For now, our focus is on understanding what happens in our bodies when we are traumatized, and as we explore that, we will need to introduce some medical terms often used by professional counselors. So bear with us for a bit as we dive into some deeper waters.

Understanding the Body's Responses

The symptoms of our bodies' responses (fight, flight, freeze, fawn) are not something we plan. They are God-ordained instincts, chemical responses that vary depending on the severity of the threat to our stability. These are knee-jerk survival mechanisms kicking in when our bodies perceive danger. We are created to believe that everything is going to be okay (or somewhat okay), and while we may survive a traumatic event, that survival means living with the feedback loops of trauma. Depending on the context and the severity of our trauma, a church, a small group, an institution, or an individual may no longer feel safe or okay for us. Again, we are designed to search for safety and love, and the experience of trauma hinges on our desire to find safety, to control the situation, and to survive the situation. When we experience trauma, we are overwhelmed and want to escape that sense of being overwhelmed. We've become unbalanced, and we are trying to become centered again and find balance because balance feels like control.

We can explain this in more detail using clinical terms. The experience of being overwhelmed relates to our bodies' forms of arousal, including both hyperarousal and hypoarousal. People who have been severely or repeatedly traumatized may lose the capacity to control higher levels of arousal. The severely traumatized often enter into a heightened state of arousal, and they may slowly lose their ability to feel safe again. Our ability to handle the various levels of arousal or our tolerance levels (referred to clinically as our allostatic load) is somewhat like trying to prevent a cup from overflowing.

When we remain in the middle of our range with our cup half filled, we are behaving and acting within our tolerance levels. We are being the type of person we want to be. We are behaving and acting in ways that we are proud of and that we desire or respect. But when our cup overflows, we respond with fight or flight, two responses that indicate a state of hyperarousal. Our cup fills up and overflows, resulting in a heightened state of awareness as we seek a way to survive. We are now ready to fight or run away from a real danger, and when we are faced with a time-limited event and are able to save ourselves, this response is very effective. This hyperarousal is commonly marked by agitation, anger, panic, irritation, and frustration.

We may also enter into hypoarousal. In this case, our cup is full of a sense of being overwhelmed and it overflows. But this time we attempt to survive not by fighting or fleeing but by freezing or fawning. Freezing is when we "play dead" or seek to be invisible, hoping the threat will just go away. Fawning is an attempt to be liked by the abuser or the threat, to get that individual on our side in order to survive. Fawning, similar to freezing, is an attempt to become less noticeable and potentially invisible. Hypoarousal is commonly associated with feeling hopeless, numb, ashamed, detached, and depressed. It cannot be stressed enough that both of these responses are normal and common bodily reactions to heightened stress and survival.

The Impact of Trauma

Consider a car crash in which two people are in the same vehicle and experience the same crash. One of them is the driver and the other is the passenger. For no apparent reason, the other car involved in the accident does a U-turn in the middle of the street and T-bones this car. Often in these incidents the passenger will experience a loss of power and control. Their body may experience hyperarousal and they will get a flush of adrenaline to fight or begin flight, but they are trapped in the passenger seat and there is nothing they can do to take action or gain control. The driver may attempt to slam on the brakes or turn the steering wheel to avoid as much of the other car as possible. The driver's body understands they are the one who is in control of the car and needs to take action. Their body often experiences hyperarousal and attempts to fight back by swerving or slamming on the brakes.

Though they experience the same traumatic event, the driver's perception and experience are often vastly different than the passenger's. The driver walks away with an experience of fear, but they were able to quickly take action and knew they would be okay. The passenger, on the other hand, may walk away with the experience of a captive bystander, having had to watch the events unfold as they happened to them without any measure of control. The passenger may experience a higher level of traumatic symptoms because of that loss of control or sense of feeling stuck.

Trauma begins with an event that is experienced as physically or emotionally life threatening or overwhelming, and that event has lasting effects on our well-being.[1] But what are the long-term effects of severe trauma? We often carry around with us the memory of that trauma everywhere we go. We are unable to return to a felt sense of safety, that things are okay in the world, or that we are going to be okay. We may no longer trust ourselves or others. We are unable to forget that something horrible happened to us, and we sit on the edge of our chairs waiting for it to happen again, waiting for the other shoe to drop. For some, the feeling is like waiting out a hurricane or other life-threatening event, sitting in our homes just waiting for the winds and water to hit us.

As we have already noted, trauma is embodied, meaning it is stored in the body's memory.[2] So when our bodies are reminded of the past—by what is commonly referred to as a trigger—they return automatically to that traumatic event. We relive the experience as if it were happening all over again. Obviously, this has a profound effect on our bodies, and it is helpful to think of trauma as a "memory problem" in the body. In one sense, our bodies are calling up a memory of a traumatic lived experience and putting us in that memory again. Since trauma is both the event and the experience, the effect on us is like being brought back to that event and experiencing it again and again.

These experiences may also be viewed as intrusive memories of past events. The now-intrusive experiences of past events seem to be triggered by emotions and sensations in the present that are associated with the past trauma.[3]

For example, let's consider Max and Annie, a couple who have gone out to eat. While they are enjoying a wonderful dinner, Max starts choking on his meal. The EMTs are called and life-saving measures are taken and thankfully Max survives. He takes a few days off from work to heal physically from the ordeal, but he doesn't take into account the emotional healing that may be needed. A few nights after that dinner, Max starts to experience anxiety when he sits down to eat again. He also experiences anxiety every time he smells coffee, which was sitting on the table when he choked, and he has difficulty wanting to sit across from his wife. He gets nervous when he hears sirens or when he sees someone with green eyes (the eye color of the EMT who performed CPR on him).

Max may not consciously make any connection between his anxiety and his choking event, but these are examples of how trauma lives in our bodies and how trauma is recalled from the past into our experience in the present as we attempt to heal. Trauma has lasting effects on our lives and our range of tolerance. It affects our spiritual health, our mental and emotional health, and our social relationships. Trauma leaves us in a heightened state of insecurity in which we lose our ability to trust ourselves and others. When we cannot trust ourselves, we cease growing and moving forward in life, and when we cannot trust others, we become incapable of living in right relationship with others, leading to loneliness and isolation. Some may experience depression; others often experience anxiety coming from the fear of reliving the trauma over and over again. True as well is that those who have lost a sense of trust at times wonder whether God even cares or whether God hears the cries of our hearts. When trust begins to fall apart, it can fall apart totally.

Trauma and the Church

Now that we better understand what trauma is and how it affects us, let's turn our attention to the church. How do we see trauma in the setting of a local church? We'll start by looking at how trauma may be affecting leaders, particularly pastors.

We are witnessing a rather surprising trend right now. There is a great deal of conversation about the Nones and Dones, those who answer the question of religious affiliation with "None" and those who say they are now officially "Done" with church. The surprise? Many pastors are joining the Nones and Dones. In fact, in a comparison of pastors and church attendees, we find a greater percentage of pastors leaving churches than we find among ordinary Christian attenders. One reason for this? Trauma.

In a survey taken in autumn 2023 by a research project called Exploring the Pandemic Impact on Congregations, researchers reported that more than 40 percent of clergy had seriously pondered leaving the ministry since 2020. More than half of them were considering leaving the pastoral ministry entirely, never to return.[4] Can you imagine what it would look like if more than half of congregants left or were even considering leaving? Even more telling is that 13 percent of pastors say they think often about resigning from their role. Many of the ordinary scales for measuring human wellness would suggest pastors are reasonably healthy, but after accounting for the effects of other factors (such as denomination, conflict, vitality, and willingness to change), these health and wellness measures are less significant in explaining the rise in clergy discontentment. It does not appear that a large percentage of clergy have suddenly become unwell or are suffering a dramatic emotional or spiritual dis-ease and then thinking about leaving.

> Rather, there are other significant factors which relate both to thoughts of leaving and wellness. Therefore, one must look elsewhere

> to understand the dynamics of why increased numbers of religious leaders are considering departures. For a clearer picture, we need to examine the changing contextual reality within the nation's faith communities.[5]

If the ordinary indicators of pastors' health have not declined noticeably in the last few years, other realities must be shaping their considerations to leave, including declining attendance, an incline in congregants' age, a growing resistance to any more postpandemic change in churches, and a decline in volunteers. More than a third of churches believe their church's future is uncertain.

So what's ticking in these pastors' hearts? We believe one key to nurturing safe churches may be found in looking at these pastors' experiences and why they are thinking of leaving. We want to be clear, this is not a book about traumatized pastors, even though we use the apostle Paul as a key example. This book is about trauma and thus is for anyone who has been traumatized in a church. This includes those who have been hurt and traumatized by church leaders, but it also includes the experiences of leaders who have themselves experienced trauma. Both of these experiences will contribute to our broader diagnosis and prescription for how best to nurture safe churches.

Add to all of this a new study concluding that what pastors and churches do—the church itself—seems to be waning in cultural and societal importance. Nearly 80 percent of Americans contend that religion is losing or has lost its influence in public life, the highest survey result in the last two decades. Fifty percent of Americans also think this decline is a "bad thing,"[6] and almost 60 percent of Americans believe religion still has a positive impact on society. Yet that same Pew study finds that they believe a person's faith puts them at odds with American culture: "Rather, many religious and nonreligious Americans say they feel that their religious beliefs put them at odds with mainstream culture, with the people around them and with the other side of the political spectrum." I recently had lunch with a pastor who told me that pastoring and "church itself" are traumatizing for people in a culture that increasingly looks down on the church.

Pastors are noticeably more willing to adapt to these new conditions than their congregants. But congregants—those good ol' church folks—don't like the new conditions and the adaptations their leaders may attempt to make to the church. People in the church have clearly been wounded by pastors and leaders in the church. There are countless instances of leaders abusing and manipulating congregants. Yet at the same time, humans being humans, another reality is just as true: Church people wound one another and their pastors. We refer to this, broadly speaking, as church conflict. Church conflict stands out amid the swirl of current concerns about the health of pastors and churches. More than 70 percent of churches in autumn 2023 were experiencing conflicts, and tellingly, "the more conflict a congregation experienced, the greater the likelihood the minister would anticipate leaving that placement."[7] Trauma is just one small step away from church conflict, so it is not surprising that when we review whether a pastor and congregation are a good fit and discover rancorous relations, these contribute to thoughts about leaving.

Good fit and good relationships make for a pastor who wants to stay. Here is a summary of the conclusion of the Hartford study: "What is positively associated with fewer thoughts of leaving is . . . being in a church with a bright outlook for the future, one that has less conflict, is more open to change and adaptation, and cultivates a [*sic*] good, healthy relationships between the members and pastor."[8]

Think too how contented a leader may feel about what she or he is most called to do and be. This sense of contentment is connected to what pastors like to do—what they are passionate about in their calling—and what congregants want from their pastor. Consider this list of what pastors like to do most:

- Walking with people during their spiritual journeys in commitment to God
- Having positive relationships with congregants ("church family")
- Worshiping and fellowshiping with one another (e.g., Sunday worship, singing together)
- Participating in outreach activities (e.g., food insecurity, antipoverty)
- Teaching Christian education/programming especially for youth/young adults
- Preaching (e.g., sermon preparation, Bible study)
- Seeing the church grow, particularly through children/youth participation[9]

Conflict arises whenever a pastor's perceived giftedness and the congregants' expectations clash. Rather than make the sweeping generalization that the church has never ever been in such a state before, I want to drill down into one issue: the reality of growing church conflict between congregants and their pastors. And in particular, I want to explore the impact of rancorous complaining, accusations, and anger that so many pastors experience almost daily. Many of these leaders are experiencing abuse and trauma.

Often when we think of how to address a problem in the church, we focus on the leaders and assume that if we get the leaders onboard, we can bring about change. It's not that simple. We live in a complex world, and the church shares in its complications. But here is something we need to consider as we think of the problem of church conflict. While leaders in a church (a category not limited to those with the title of pastor or minister) are the ones most responsible for nurturing, and have the greatest opportunity to nurture, safe spaces and a church safe from trauma and traumatizing, in many instances the leaders themselves have suffered their own share of traumatizing events. So we need to ask those traumatized leaders what can be done to prevent trauma. Some of their experiences, taken together with stories of traumatized congregants, have led us to propose four elements we need to nurture to cultivate a trauma-safe environment in the church. In the end, it really doesn't matter who did what to whom. Our goal is to learn from any experience of trauma how to make our churches safe.

Bottom-Up Abuse

The abuse congregants and others suffer by the hands of pastors and those with spiritual power and authority (the sort one finds in Ezekiel 34, 2 Peter 2, and Jude, for example) has been studied extensively. Much of it has been made even worse by careless comments, muckrakers tossing out thoughtless tweets. The culture formed around abusive pastors and the trail left behind them in damaged relationships and distorted church cultures has also been examined and exposed. My (Scot) daughter, Laura Barringer, and I have written two books on this topic, one detailing stories of abuse and another that maps a way out of toxic church culture.[10] But very little has been done to take into account the reality of toxic church people abusing pastors and church leaders, both women and men. Even less has been written about the impact of abusive congregations on the spouses of pastors who have been targeted. Our hope is that this study will compel some additional work in this area.

Our goal is to consider any experience of trauma in the church—to look at the problems found in a traumatized church, among both congregants and leaders. At times, congregants' behaviors traumatize their pastor. Here are several brief examples to consider:

- A coalition within a church was formed to oppose several significant decisions made by the pastor. A longtime staff member who had always supported the pastor opposed the coalition. As so often happens in churches, word leaked out that this staff member had criticized members of the coalition. The coalition, behind closed doors, scapegoated the staff member with unsubstantiated gossip and slander. The pastor, sensing the direction this turbulence was headed, joined the coalition against his former colleague. Traumatized by this betrayal, the staff member resigned and searched for work outside a church, vowing he'd never work in a church again. Here we have an instance of congregational abuse of a staff member leading to trauma—or to put it more simply, Christians abusing other Christians. It doesn't matter that some of the actors were pastors or that the traumatized person was a leader within the church; what matters is that abuse occurred and trauma was the result.
- A female associate pastor with considerable abilities in teaching who drew numerous people to her adult Bible studies had to make two difficult personnel decisions. Disagreeing with her, a powerful man on staff with a history of disliking other leaders began plotting against the associate pastor behind closed doors with a part-time female staff member and several congregants. They spread gossip and began passing on anything negative they learned about the female pastor. For her part, the associate pastor had no idea any of this was happening until another staff member divulged the plotting against her. She was severely traumatized when she realized several of her coworkers in ministry had pretended to support and affirm her, and she experienced a profound sense of betrayal. She soon resigned and accepted a job working for a publisher, where she now flourishes. Again, we have an example of Christians traumatizing other Christians.

- A former intern at a church leveled accusations against a former associate in ministry who had attempted to care for the intern. The former intern was dissatisfied with how the associate responded, even though the associate offered an apology. The intern then chose to criticize his former associate on Facebook in detail. Hundreds of former congregants read one false accusation after another, all stemming from attempts by the associate to care for their former intern. Not only can social media go viral but the virality of the comments can wound in ways simple conversations never can. In many cases, pastors have watched their congregants pile on with negative criticism. Criticism on social media routinely traumatizes pastors. The one who wrote me about this instance added, "It is eye-opening that people you pour so much into can also cause you so much harm and pain." Church folks traumatizing other church folks.

Religious trauma is more common than you might think. Our Bible may not describe the people we meet in its pages in modern, psychological terms. The Bible may not use affective terms for those who are wounded, but it doesn't change the reality that trauma happened then just as it does today.

Over the past five years, knowing my (Scot) advocacy for those who have experienced spiritual abuse and the abuse of power at the hands of church leaders, many people have written to me or discussed with me over coffee the abuse they have experienced from other Christians. And in my study of Scripture, I've found an unexpected example of this in the apostle Paul's life and in his relationship with one of the early churches. You may be surprised (we certainly were) to learn how neatly the apostle Paul fits into the model of people who have been abused by other Christians, as we will soon see. We are not attempting to turn Paul into the model of a traumatized leader. He's not. But we do think we can learn about trauma in the church from Paul because he was himself traumatized by other Christians.

The Politics of the Pandemic

Nothing in our history has complicated relationships among Christians like the COVID-19 pandemic has, tossed as it was into a decade-long fraught and frightening set of political elections. Pew sitters, volunteers, and pastors experienced conflict over candidates and masks. Some left, some stayed for the fight, and some survived. We have heard almost no stories of how the faith of a community flourished and grew, and even among those who did, there were still battle scars and broken relationships.

Here's one pastor's story:

> As I made my way around to the different campsites, saying goodbye with fist bumps and hugs, I did not know that this would be our final churchwide camping trip together. It would also be the last time that I would ever see more than half of my congregants again. It was March 2020, and the elders and I had, along with most churches, opted to cancel Sunday services. But by the second week my voice mail and inbox were already filling up with letters from zealous parishioners asking us to reconsider halting our Sunday gatherings. I took the time to address each one, trying to calm their fears, but they kept coming. The emails turned into phone calls, then into video meetings, each incoming reply more tinged with anger and political ideology than the last. No matter how hard I tried to de-escalate, the temperature kept going up. And once the anger started flowing, it didn't stop for almost a year and a half.

Leading a church through the pandemic pressed leadership teams, elders, and deacons, as well as ordinary people tasked with a new responsibility: How do you present information about the pandemic and wisely guide the church through such an unprecedented event? Many leaders found themselves in places they never expected to be or having conversations they never expected to have. Politics played handsy with pastors who sought peace among their people, with some pushing for one strategy and then meeting pushback from the other side. Many leaders gave in to appease the loudest voices while others just gave up. But masking or ZoomChurch were never the primary issue. The real issues were concerns about freedom and safety and science and conspiracies and politics and personal opinions. Good church folk, taught from day one to keep the peace and absorb the hits, were now overwhelmed and burned out. Many remain traumatized by what occurred during those years.

The pastor's story continues:

> The church where I have served for two decades had always been a politically diverse gathering. We'd survived the first three divisive years of the Trump administration relatively intact and unified, not just because we were able to acknowledge our differences of opinion gracefully but because the communion table that we shared every week gave us an opportunity to look each other in the eye and affirm that the body of Christ had been broken, and the blood of Christ poured out, for each of us. The strength of our church was its unity through the communion table, but it also turned out to be our Achilles heel. The pandemic was almost diabolical in its ability to break apart our church community through removing the practice of communion. Sermons, prayers, songs, and liturgies can sometimes offend, but the table heals, and COVID had removed our ability to take communion together and, therefore, our ability to hold common space for each other, and so division set in.

We remained online until January 2021, when we reopened at 25 percent capacity. I was met by another flood of emails and phone calls making demands, often with threats and personal attacks. My conservative parishioners were fed up that we had waited so long to open, and even more so that we weren't fully opening the building back up at 100 percent capacity. A couple who once credited our church with saving their marriage now used words like fascist and Marxist to describe me. Another whom we had walked with out of a crippling heroin addiction years earlier now called me a tool of leftist propaganda. But it wasn't just the conservatives anymore. My progressive parishioners were now lashing out as well, appalled that we would have physical gatherings at all—no matter the social distancing or mask requirements. The elders and I had fallen under the inspection of a microscope so powerful that no one could endure it. Suddenly our justice work wasn't enough, our church wasn't safe enough, nothing was enough.

I could no longer measure up to the measuring stick the social-media algorithms had created within them.

I am amazed how quickly people will turn situations into symbols of the ruling political tensions. A pastoral decision made with oceans of prayer following conversations with informed people and wise counselors is interpreted as a politically prompted platform, one to combat with slurs, slogans, and slanders. It's an environment ripe for church conflict and trauma. And many have suffered or experienced trauma in recent years, though they may not realize it.

So how do we recognize whether someone has experienced it? What are the symptoms of trauma? In the next chapter we'll learn how to recognize trauma for what it is, especially when it is the result of spiritual abuse in the church.

Chapter 3

Trauma's Symptoms

What does diagnosable trauma look like? It would be too theoretical to begin with our bodies' neurological and biological responses because most of us don't have the skill to diagnose them. So we'll begin with the real story of a traumatized person who had the skill to articulate what happens to a person in the trauma zone. The person sharing happens to have been a senior pastor at a church when these events occurred.

> It was our third Sunday back [from the pandemic] when things changed. This was the first time I noticed that something was happening inside of me, right in the center of my chest. That evening we had a couple of old friends over to our front porch to connect with us. As I listened to them recount the words of disgruntled congregants, something broke. My heart began to beat faster and faster. I closed my eyes and tried to breathe through it, trying not to draw attention, but I couldn't slow it. My muscles started to buzz all over as if I was running out of oxygen.
>
> I looked at my wife in a panic. She immediately came to me, lifted one of my arms over her shoulder and started to walk me inside

asking, "What's wrong?" "Don't talk; don't say anything," I said. "I have to get to the bed." Breathing heavily, I was starting to see colors that weren't there as she laid me on the bed. I fell asleep.

I had never had a panic attack before, nor have I had anything like it since. But this event marked a change in my physical responses. I noticed that my fight-or-flight reflex began to fire whenever I received email or DM notifications. My body would get hot, and I would start pacing the room, as if ready to run away. I could no longer sleep when the sun went down; my body was hypervigilant; the slightest sound would wake me up. I resorted to naps during the day, often working at night.

Many of these symptoms have since subsided, but some have become a part of my daily routine, such as the deep breaths I must take before opening my inbox to control my heart rate.

This account accurately describing trauma was spurred by a friend sharing information about people who were unhappy about things at their church. The pastor hearing this perceived it as threatening information, even though the words that were shared with him did not threaten his body or his life. But at another level, this information threatened something else, perhaps his ability to lead unhappy individuals. Maybe the threat he perceived was the potential for a split in the church, something he had been worried about. His body and emotions also may have been taxed, since this was shortly after the pandemic lockdowns. The threat—whatever it may have been—was felt in his body, and he was not able to get ahead of it, nor could he relax or calm down. Once his body had begun reacting to the words that were shared with him, the threat in his body became real, with telltale signs of shortness of breath and a pounding heart rate.

One way traumatized believers have learned to respond is to turn to the Scriptures, often looking to figures like Job or Jeremiah as guides.

In addition, many will turn to spiritual directors, mentors, or therapists. Others turn to those who have undergone similar experiences. But I don't often hear people mention the apostle Paul as a source of understanding and comfort. We may forget that Paul begins the letter we call 2 Corinthians with clear indications that he is in deep pain. He says, "We were depressed—excessively, beyond ability [to cope, no doubt]—so that we despaired even of living," and he speaks of this pain as a "death sentence" (1:8–9). And then in chapter 4, he reflects on his condition yet again: "In every way, [we are] ones being troubled but not distressed; ones perplexed but not overperplexed, ones being chased but not abandoned, ones being tossed down but not destroyed" (4:8–9). After listing all of his physical sufferings during his mission work, Paul turns to his inner world, noting that "there is my daily supervision, [that is], the anxiety for all the assemblies" (11:28). Depression and anxiety often join chambers in the heart of the traumatized.

It may surprise you, but I'll say it again: Paul is someone the traumatized Christian can identify with. In describing Paul's response to the Corinthian church, Peter Yuichi Clark says this letter "offers a testimony of his human journey through illness, with an emerging awareness of his own vulnerability, and it illustrates how relying on the power of divine grace has led him (and, by extension, can lead us) toward healing and wholeness."[1] Far too many have passed over, have minimized, and are (sorry to say it this way) utterly tone deaf to Paul's pain as they seek to explain his theology and his responses to the Corinthians. But if we linger over his words, we may experience some precious moments of connection with him that help us better understand his heart. A pained heart it is. Paul was spiritually abused by the people in Corinth—some who claimed to be leaders, of course—but the letters also indicate that there were entire segments of those house churches—what we might call congregants—that also detested Paul.

In the last five years or so I (Scot) have listened to hundreds of stories about spiritual abuse in churches, some at the hand of pastors and leaders, but others doled out by fellow congregants. But almost no one points such persons to the intensely personal chapters detailing church conflict in 2 Corinthians 10–13. Those who have looked into those chapters have found something interesting. I've been told things like "Paul felt what I feel" and "I have never thought of Paul living with me in the trauma zone." All types of people experience spiritual abuse: congregants, leaders, and everyone in between. As I hope you are seeing in the examples we've shared so far, many leaders have experienced spiritual abuse in churches from their peers.

However, since we're now using the word *spiritual* with abuse, let's pause for a short explanation of this term to make sure we're all on the same page before moving ahead.

Symptoms of Spiritual Abuse

Spiritual trauma, which has special emphasis in this book, deserves its own set of descriptions in addition to those of a more general experience of trauma. Just as general trauma dismantles a person's sense of safety, security, and well-being, spiritual trauma may dismantle a person's view of the world, God, themselves, their faith, their community, and their church. Those who have been spiritually traumatized cannot but be on the constant alert for wounding words and behaviors in churches.

What then is spiritual abuse? Spiritual abuse occurs when a person with religious authority abuses another person in the context of a spiritual relationship. The power is asymmetrical. The irony is that in some instances a congregation, or a group within a congregation, can be the one wielding that power, spiritually abusing other members and even leaders in the church. This is possible because in some church structures and communities, congregational power can (ironically) become asymmetrical to a pastor's own power. The story that began this chapter reveals an example of asymmetrical power wielded by a power bloc in a church that turned against the pastor himself. This is why we cannot limit our understanding of spiritual abuse to congregants alone. We need to consider a well-researched study by Lisa Oakley and Justin Humphreys, who define spiritual abuse as follows (reformatted for clarity in reading):

> Spiritual abuse is a form of emotional and psychological abuse.
>
> It is characterized by a systematic pattern of coercive and controlling behavior in a religious context.
>
> Spiritual abuse can have a deeply damaging impact on those who experience it.
>
> This abuse may include manipulation and exploitation, enforced accountability, censorship of decision making, requirements for secrecy and silence, coercion to conform, [inability to ask questions] control through the use of sacred texts or teaching, requirement of obedience to the abuser, the suggestion that the abuser has a "divine" position, isolation as a means of punishment, and superiority and elitism.[2]

Randal Rauser and Bob Stenhouse, both Canadians, one a theologian and the other a former detective who has become a specialist in abuse investigations, have extensively studied spiritual abuse, and they accurately contend that spiritual abuse can occur in relationships other than instances when an established spiritual authority, such as a pastor, seeks to control and wound (traumatize) another person. They give examples of spiritual abuse in the following five relational situations:

1. A pastor's son possessing indirect, but real, power
2. The wealthiest donor in a church throwing around the power of money

3. An assertive personality forcing his or her way in a situation
4. A person who claims to know God's will in a direct manner
5. Someone who knows the Bible who can overpower those who don't know the Bible well[3]

To be clear, spiritual abuse is real, leaving wounds and trauma in its wake. In the proposal brought by Rauser and Stenhouse (which reflects the cultural context of Canada), spiritual abuse occurs as "harassment, bullying, sexual harassment" and also comes into their definition as "the abusive exercise of coercive power and control in a spiritual context often in a manner that humiliates, demoralizes, and/or terrorizes another."[4] They further describe spiritual abuse as a form of emotional abuse, which is "a pattern of behavior in which the perpetrator insults, humiliates, and generally instills fear in an individual in order to control them." Thus, it "centers around control, manipulation, isolation, and demeaning or threatening behavior."[5]

So while we tend to think of pastors or leaders as those who spiritually abuse others, if we broaden our scope to include family members, donors, assertive personalities, and those with special claims to knowing God or knowing the authority of the Bible as examples of people in positions of spiritual power or authority, we expand our understanding of potential instances of trauma in the church to include interactions between lay members, congregants, and segments or groups within a congregation. These individuals and groups can become abusive as well. Even some churches have collectively become systemically abusive of anyone who criticizes them or offers them suggestions.

A traumatized person, whoever it might be and at whatever level they exist within a Christian organization's hierarchy, experiences heightened awareness. This is a sense of feeling the need to be totally alert, something experts refer to as hypervigilance. Their system of self-preservation goes into immediate, constant alert, as if the danger could appear at any moment and they cannot know how long it may last.[6] Many have compiled lists of indicators that a person is in the trauma zone with a body struggling with emotional dysregulation, and they include anxiety and depression, as well as struggles with one's relationships, digestive disorders, and even obsessive-compulsive symptoms. Above all, the acronym PTSD (post-traumatic stress disorder) classifies a person who has experienced trauma. We have met many leaders who have symptoms of PTSD, and later in this book we will look at an apostle who may well have the same diagnosis.

We can further complicate our understanding of spiritual abuse and trauma by looking at it from another angle: how a traumatized person responds to their trauma and how they respond to those who have hurt them. A traumatized person can be angry and stunned by fear, and may find it difficult to trust others, especially persons like the one who traumatized them. They often find it difficult to trust their own diagnoses of themselves. They experience dysregulation and become agitated, anxious, angry, and/or confused. Trauma affects our ability to attach, both to other individuals and to communities.[7] Let's dig a little deeper into how traumatized persons respond to those who traumatized them.

Responses to Trauma

As we mentioned earlier, studies have shown that traumatized persons respond to trauma in a pattern summed up by four terms beginning with the letter *F*: fight, flight, freeze, fawn. We'll take some time now to explain them more completely.

These terms not only describe the responses of the traumatized but can also be clear indicators of the presence of trauma in a person. Those with ears that listen and eyes that observe will see these responses and learn to recognize a person who is in trauma.

Hyperarousal Responses

Fight and flight are classed by some as hyperarousal states, very excited states.

Fight

A natural hyperarousal response of a human body to a threat is to fight back: The person lashes out, powers up, and even attempts to intimidate the person or situation threatening their safety. Fighting can occur not only with the arms and legs and strength but also with words (spoken or written), yelling, and screaming for help. The person's face displays the response of fighting.

Flight

If a person cannot fight, a common response is flight. One protects oneself from the threat by fleeing the situation—physically getting away, professionally resigning, or emotionally withdrawing, for example.

Hypoarousal Responses

The next two responses are called hypoarousal states—instances when a person's emotions are suppressed or depressed.

A threatened, traumatized person enters hypoarousal in the sense that the person tunes out their thoughts and feelings, shutting down. If hyperarousal's symptom is anxiety, hypoarousal's symptom may be depression or numbness, a sense of being physically but not emotionally present. I've witnessed the latter with a pastor preaching when he was not emotionally present. Words were spoken, but no body, soul, life, or feelings were attached to the words.

Freeze

To freeze is to become immobile and possibly incapable of moving; the person is stunned, standing there unable to decide, unable even to do anything. At times a person enters into an extended freezing called dissociation, where the person's mind leaves the body. (I [Scot] believe one needs to understand dissociation to better understand some who are considered to be demon possessed. One needs also to understand multiple personality disorders, but these are topics worth exploring by someone else.)

Since this book will not delve into Paul as an example of someone who froze in the trauma zone, we will spend more time looking at freezing here. Consider, as an example, a woman who has been sexually abused or assaulted. Rauser and Stenhouse's study insightfully proposes that we understand freezing as "tonic immobility," something that "occurs when a person is placed within a high stress situation, and they respond by dissociating from the situation or even becoming physically immobilized" or when the person "becomes compliant with the wishes of the perpetrator." The authors of the study add the important insight that "these responses can be mistaken for consent." They continue, "The unifying theme within tonic immobility responses is that the person withdraws into compliance or inaction as a defense response."[8] What can be seen as immobility and compliance, or mistakenly as participation, happens as way of self-protection and defense.

Freezing as tonic immobility overlaps substantially with fawning.

Fawn

To fawn is to surrender to the abuser, to capitulate, or to give in. A fawning person gives up any desire to fight or flee and instead seeks to have the abuser like them by making themselves more appealing. Many abused women have coped with trauma by fawning. However, it is important to see this as a way of coping and should not be confused with codependency. Earlier, we shared a story of a missionary woman whose response to her husband's ongoing abuse was fawning.

Why have we reviewed these four responses to trauma? Because to understand how people respond to trauma, we need to recognize that traumatized people can strike back in ways that traumatize others. Just because someone is traumatized doesn't mean they are innocent of all wrong. As we will see, Paul's tone, harshness, sarcasm, and irony, as well as the labels he uses in his letters to the Corinthians, can be explained insightfully through the lens of trauma. However, being traumatized doesn't justify vehemency or labeling your critics as evil and demonic. Ironically, Paul seems to be aware of what he's doing—lashing out, defending himself, flipping terms upside down—while doing his best to say he's not doing what they think he's doing. He knows what his critics are thinking. His emotions are visible and expressed, and this is important because a traumatized person's suppression of anger can jeopardize that person's emotional well-being. At the same, becoming unhinged or lashing out at others jeopardizes everything, complicating relationships while traumatizing the targets of one's anger. Church relationships—like any relationship—can be exceedingly complicated and, because of those complications, the traumatized persons are typically not the ones who diagnose the problems or the solutions.

Let's see whether we can apply this insight by listening to the apostle Paul's vulnerable expressions. In the next section, we'll look closely at Paul, his relationship with the Corinthian church, and the very real pain he experienced in that relationship. We'll see how he felt, how he responded, and how his erratic responses can best be explained by understanding him to be in the trauma zone.

PART 2

Trauma Sensitive

THE EARS

Chapter 4

Listening to a Backstory

P. D. James, in her mystery novel *Death in Holy Orders*, records a conversation between detective Dalgliesh and Mrs. Pilbeam. Mrs. Pilbeam is being asked to read from Scripture during a funeral service, and upon hearing that it is a reading from the apostle Paul, she tells the priest, Father Sebastian, what she thinks of the apostle.

> Father Sebastian thought I might like to read a passage from St. Paul, but I said I'd rather just say a prayer instead. Somehow I can't take St. Paul. Seems to me he was a bit of a troublemaker. There were those little groups of Christians all minding their own business and getting along all right, by and large. No one's perfect. And then St. Paul arrives unexpectedly and starts bossing and criticizing. Or he'd send them one of his fierce letters. Not the kind of letter I'd care to receive, and so I told Father Sebastian.[1]

Ignoring the fact that Paul did not invade churches already formed but planted his own, perhaps P. D. James is after Paul for other reasons. And maybe you find yourself agreeing with Mrs. Pilbeam. We are more than aware that many have no time for the man, thinking he's not just bossy but a chauvinist and an authoritarian, maybe even showing some hints of narcissism. Others, on the other hand, adore the man and his ideas. One of my doctoral students opened a chapter in his thesis with this statement: "It took nine years of theological education before I realized the apostle Paul might not be a total jerk. I remember making an offhand remark about Paul in my first doctoral seminar, where I referred to Paul as an aggressive jerk. Instead of getting a laugh of agreement, I received a look like I had just insulted the professor's best friend." I'll go on record now to reveal I was that professor. That student's thesis was, ironically, a model thesis exploring friendship, and over the course of his studies Paul had become one of his friends.

In the chapters that follow I hope we can, at the very least, show you that Paul was vulnerable, less than certain about some of his decisions, and, yes, a deeply wounded man. There are several passages in his letters that, if he were sharing them today with a therapist, might get him diagnosed as traumatized or perhaps even PTSD.

But even more than that, and here I (Scot) speak from my own experience working with wounded church folks, when I have spoken on the subject of Paul and trauma, I've seen church leaders weeping over Paul's pain, seeing some of that pain in themselves. What we can learn from Paul is how the traumatized feel, how they respond, and how others treat them when they express their wounds. At certain times in his letters, Paul provides a clear window into someone who is in the trauma zone. If we read Paul carefully, it can better help us understand what trauma does to a person.

Yes, Paul is an apostle. He's unlike you and me in countless ways. But he is like us in several others. First, he was a human being exercising the gift God had given him. Yet he was not a local pastor or even a local leader, and what authority he had was temporary as he planted the church. When Paul left the church, some of the leaders who took over more or less did what they wanted to do. Paul was like us in ways that matter deeply. Think of him the way you may think of yourself, as a Christian doing what God has called you to do. And then think of the withering criticisms he endured, which we will canvass in this book, and imagine yourself in the same position. We'd all be traumatized by what he experienced.

I am encouraged by a growing trend of exploring what we know about trauma and the connection between our bodies, minds, and emotions, and how that can aid us in understanding characters in the Bible and theology (and even theologians). Recently, Michelle Keener explores how the book of Job reveals a traumatized man.[2] (How could he not be!) Her book is a wonderful example of how serious Bible readers can make use of trauma theory as a contributing factor in reading the Bible. And if anyone still has doubt as to the value of this endeavor, let me ask you to read Job's first chapter and then ask yourself this question: What emotions would Job have felt after experiencing the loss of everything he loved and so much of what he knew to be home? Then, if you have the heart for it, read Job's responses, both to God and to his friends, in this very long book of the Bible, but read them as the responses of a traumatized person. I know Michelle's book helped me to move beyond reading the book of Job as simply a philosophical treatise about the arbitrary nature of events and pain and evil. It helped me empathize with Job in ways I did not before. Helen Paynter, who specializes in the study of the Bible and violence, endorsed Michelle's book with these words: "Above all, this book sings of a scripture that is sensitive to survivors of trauma, and a God who meets them in the ashes." In a similar way, we believe Paul is working through his own trauma and pain in several passages in 2 Corinthians.

The Importance of the Backstory

A student and I were talking, and she expressed some anger about the subject we were discussing, which seemed appropriate. We continued the conversation. She then got angry about a similar topic. We continued. Once again, same topic, same anger. At this point, I made a facial gesture hinting to her that maybe she was too angry over this topic, commenting that people can handle only so much anger. She looked me straight in the eye and from a position of clarity and confidence said, "I'm angry. I deserve to be. It's okay to be angry."

Then she told me her story.

What she had experienced at the hand of male leaders in a church had traumatized her. Her backstory helped me to understand why she was justifiably angry. I learned that the male students she encountered in class reminded her of the male abusers in her life. Her backstory explained why she frequently got heated over classmates who were acting "manly" about themselves and in the way they treated other women in her class. And she was angry, as well, over their mansplaining theology.

Backstories matter. For more than a decade I have taught in a seminary with an above-average number of female students. And I have been surprised by how many of these women have suffered at the hands of both congregants and pastoral leaders. Their backstories often come through in their responses in our class discussions, in their lunchtime conversations with classmates, and in evenings spent together.

I saw several of their backstories at work in a different class taught by a colleague covering a popular concept in biblical studies, cruciformity (being formed by the cross). One way to think of it is the imitation of Christ's suffering in this world. Sometimes it's called redemptive suffering, though at times this can sound like being asked to take one for the team. Some have even labeled it redemptive violence because for women (and men) with an abuse backstory, cruciformity sounds like a legitimatization of violence. Some of our students react to the term cruciformity with anger and anxiety, and several have exhibited symptoms of trauma during our discussions and have had to leave the room.

The reality of life is that divisions happen among Christians and there are, sadly, tragic incidents of real abuse and violence covered over with religious justifications. Some of this we will find in the church at Corinth, which will become a central character in the stories we examine as we walk through the surprisingly uber-relevant life of the apostle Paul in the trauma zone. In later chapters, we will look more closely at the topic of cruciformity/Christoformity, and at that point will use the term positively to describe how the apostle Paul responded at times to the trauma he experienced. When we do so, know that I am doing the best I can to remain trauma sensitive to those who think *cruciformity* needs serious nuancing.

The Most Important Element of a Backstory: Listening

We all need to listen. We may know how to listen, but that doesn't mean we are all good listeners. Listening is an art. If you were to rifle through your memories and find a good conversation, what would you remember about that time together? Did it feel different in some way? Most likely you felt seen, heard, and understood. The art of listening requires skills, skills that are especially important when we are listening to narratives about trauma. These skills include attunement, empathy, open-mindedness, protection, and even deep breathing. We all need to learn these skills to some degree, because they are expressions of the respectful love of one person for another.

Attunement is the act of giving our full attention to someone so as to connect with that person, both by listening and engaging with them.

We make eye contact. We turn our face toward the other person's face. Attunement brings our facial expressions into harmony with what the person tells us. This is a highly active process involving our bodies, our minds, and our words. Connecting to someone forms a relationship with another person and in doing so reveals that they have been understood. Some clinicians call attunement "mutual delight," the shared experience of belonging and being heard. Attunement engages with another person's story so we can know more about the person.

When a trauma is shared with us, we give the survivor the opportunity to put their story in order. Traumas involve a sequence: a start, a middle, and an end. A story told in order empowers a trauma survivor to make meaning of their story. Attunement, then, provides space for a person to tell their story, knowing that we hear them and that they are being heard.

The art of listening also involves empathy. Empathy, similar to attunement, involves listening to another person's story. But in showing empathy we also strive to hear their story not through our ears but through theirs. Empathy seeks to feel what the other person feels and connects us to their experience. Their story, even if the story follows the script of a common story of abuse, is their story and is unique to them. We may sense their story is one that has played out dozens of times, but not for them. Their story, their feelings, and their experiences are unique and valid because they happened to them. Empathy validates their feelings, their experiences, and their story, and the skill of empathy in listening attunes us to someone else so we can hear their story told through their words.

Open-mindedness goes hand in hand with empathy. People in the trauma zone may do some really weird or strange things, preventing them from sharing their stories with others. They do not always understand why they did or did not do something. Why didn't they scream louder? Why didn't they say no at the very beginning? Why did they run away but not tell anyone for years? Often they do not know the answer to these questions, and the shame and guilt they feel eats at them. Open-mindedness is a skill in listening to those in the trauma zone because we can't predict what others might do. Attunement, empathy, and open-mindedness in listening validate their experience. We inform them that it is okay that they responded as they did. That it is okay to feel ashamed or frustrated. We may inform them that what they did may never make sense. We listen not as a judge or a jury does with the goal of rendering a decision. We listen so that the storyteller knows she or he has been heard.

Listening with empathy and open-mindedness has often been miscorrelated with agreement and taking sides. We may be internally asking ourselves, Do I buy this story? Does it make any sense? If I let them continue and I don't argue, does it mean I am believing everything they say? The art of listening with empathy and open-mindedness does not mean we agree with what they say. It means we hear them, we care for them, and we step into their pain.

But what if the storyteller, after they have told us their story, asks, "Do you believe what I am telling you?" It is okay to say, "I have heard everything you shared and it sounds like that is how you saw all of this happening to you and around you. I believe this is how you remember the actions or events, and right now that is what matters." Again, listening with empathy and open-mindedness does not mean we agree with the storyteller's story. We may agree, we may not agree, and we most likely will believe most of what they share.

The art of listening also involves protection. We need to take care of ourselves when we are working with or involved with someone's trauma story. Trauma leaves its mark on everyone involved in ways big and small—including the active listener. Listeners of trauma stories can enter into what is called "vicarious trauma." Vicarious trauma comes from bearing witness to another's suffering, as listening to trauma leaves its mark on us. Being aware of vicarious trauma brings an awareness that we, as listeners, need to care for ourselves while caring for others. Many may not know this, but therapists may experience nightmares and flashbacks they themselves did not experience but are mental images someone else shared with them. Vicarious trauma can also shape how we as listeners see the world and how we choose to engage in it. It can make us wary of people or places. Vicarious trauma may (even unconsciously) lead us to avoid scenarios.

I (Adrienne) started working with traumatized children long before I had children of my own. I cannot count how many stories of trauma I had heard by the time my children were little. My experience of vicarious trauma prevented me from allowing my children to go to the restroom alone in fast-food places that had children's play areas. Though my family had never had a negative personal experience with the bathrooms in fast-food restaurants, many of those who had shared their stories with me did. Because of this my children were never allowed into those restrooms alone. Vicarious trauma shaped me as a parent and affected my choices.

One of the most powerful things a listener can do when trauma or pain is being shared with them is to take slow deep breaths. When we are living in relaxed bodies, with no tense muscles and taking deep breaths, our heart rates slow down. The simple act of deep breathing within our bodies communicates to our brains that we are safe and there is no threat. When we feel safe, the person we are listening to may even detect our safety, and our facial expressions will create safety for the storyteller as well. As we listen to a story that can feel threatening and scary, we are present and living in a body that is safe. That safety helps us to stay fully present and attuned with the individual in their experience, no matter how difficult the story is to hear.[3] We can even pass this practice on to those to whom we are listening. We can ask them to relax their muscles and to take some slow deep breaths.

If we see them getting agitated and worked up, their senses becoming heightened like they are reliving the moment, we can press the pause button and ask them to take some deep breaths. Trauma shared in a tense, threatened body often retraumatizes the person. Sharing trauma can create a sense of validation and understanding, but this can take place only if they are not reliving the trauma—if they are relaxed. So when we as listeners relax our bodies and take deep breaths, we invite the storyteller to match our relaxation and regulation. Our relaxed bodies can help them relax, regulate, and feel safe.

The Backstory: More Now Than Then

As I (Scot) spent time studying and researching the correspondence between Paul and the Corinthians, I found that Adrienne's work on trauma gave me ears to hear things I had not heard previously. Knowing that the skill of listening is vital to understanding a person in the trauma zone, I became aware that I was not fully listening to Paul's words. So what was Paul's backstory? What led to his traumatic conflict with the Corinthians?

We know that some of the church folks in Corinth preferred Apollos or Peter over Paul, while others were committed to Paul as their pastoral guide.[4] Factions arose and, as in all factional divisions, each side knew with certainty it was right. Some today think the divisions in Corinth were reducible to two main factions: Paul versus Apollos. The presence of Peter in that famous set of lines in the first chapter of 1 Corinthians has convinced others that there were three, perhaps even four, factions: "I am of Paulos" and "I am of Apollos" and "I am of Kephas [Cephas]" and "I am of Christos" (1:12). One way of reading what Paul means in highlighting these four names is that some were committed to Paul, while those who wanted eloquence were for

Apollos, and those who preferred the ways of Peter to Paul liked the former. Others, either wanting to transcend these skirmishes between leaders or wanting to get back to Jesus' teachings, claimed they were following just Jesus. It was a gaggle of personality cults.

When divisions in a Christian organization arise, someone always claims the high ground by saying the others are divisive. But disagreement, as is often expressed by Paul in his letters, cannot be simply equated with divisiveness. The person claiming high ground may claim even higher ground by quoting words from Jesus' prayer in John 17:11: "Holy Father, protect them by the power of your name, the name you gave me, so that they may be one as we are one" (NIV). Blanketing disagreements with the claim to take the high ground can often become a plea for uniformity, but uniformity is not unity. Uniformity is coercive and top down, which often effectively means silencing and suppressing those who disagree. The unity for which Jesus prays recognizes differences, disagreements, and diversity, but the unity of being siblings in Christ transcends all of those *D* words.

If one wants to simplify the problems in Corinth, they can be reduced to a desire for power, which can be loosely equated with status or honor. What was then is what is now, right? Not only did these standard human self-preoccupations matter in Corinth because they mattered in Rome, but these terms have always played out in a zero-sum game. There were those who got the power and glory, and those who did not. Divisive people want control, craving power, wanting status, desiring honor and authority, with that final word often emerging in discussions behind closed doors. Discord and disruption are the games played to get the power. They seek power over others, domination, even when the wielders of power wash it with a sanctified theology of "for God is not a God of disorder" (1 Cor. 14:33 NIV) or "anarchy."

The origin of many disruptions among Christians is a grievance, perhaps a wounding of the ego or a personal slight. Someone with authority claims too much authority and chooses a direction someone else doesn't want to go. Someone complains. Grudges form. In retaliation, however smooth in words or indirect in works, they claim the high ground of freedom. Ironically, such appeals to freedom from authority often come from those who themselves want to have authority to silence others. Other allegations arise, and terms like *autocrat* and *tyrant* become the watchwords, words that, once used, stick unjustly to the leader.

In our experience, those who gripe the most about "too much power" are those who want that power. And one method disrupters use is indirection: A leader in the band of resistance gets others to do the dirty work of expressing the allegations. They want power, but they don't want the responsibility of having caused the disorder. That's because the power desired by the disrupters is fleshly and unspiritual, and the acquisition of power justifies whatever means is necessary to obtain it. Virtue and this kind of disruption cannot hold hands.

Cliques and coalitions form, as they did in Corinth around Apollos and Peter, though we have no idea whether either of them stirred the pot. It would be hard not to. The clique's goal is to undermine those in authority, so the clique's leader gathers those who have been shaped into a famous line: "An enemy of my enemy is a friend." Gossip bites are dropped in meetings, in casual conversations, and over coffee. Those who bite on the gossip join the clique, and before long the leaders perceive something amok. Their leadership becomes a struggle to lead. In nearly all such experiences of divisiveness, the core tension points become political. Minor issues become major problems that can be wedges separating siblings in Christ. Sides form over the wedge issues. The director released my friend. The supervisor chose that person over me, but instead of saying "over me," the complainant gives an excuse to take the high road and says "without considering seniority." If we had the mind of God, we would better perceive the malice that often drives these wedge issues.

Someone always leads these divisions with a narrative, and that story takes hold of the group. The leader is the aggrieved and takes it upon himself or herself to represent the aggrieved. Leaders who have narcissistic tendencies are charming and charismatic, but they are fundamentally shaped by a deep sense of shame. Hence, they cannot absorb failure or criticism, and are therefore marked by selfishness, entitlement, a lack of empathy, restlessness and inconsistency, a regular use of others for the agenda, and, frequently, a hypersensitivity to even the slightest of criticisms. They need a constant supply of admiration and glory from those on their side. A narcissist may attempt to love bomb those he wants in his inner circle or surround himself with those who admire him, are faithful to him, and will become sycophants. He or she may flout the rules, the procedures, and fundamental Christian or civil decency, knocking down anyone acquiring any of his glory. When the narcissistic leader hears criticisms, he or she either pushes the critic out of the inner circle or flips the criticism upside down so that it is targeted at the critic (often referred to as DARVO: deny, attack, reverse victim and offender). An expert on narcissism, Ramani Durvasula, defines narcissism like this: "Narcissism is about a deep insecurity and fragility offset by maneuvers like domination, manipulation, and gaslighting, which allow the narcissistic person to stay in control. The variable empathy and lack of self-awareness mean that they do not stop to consider the harm their behavior is creating for other people."[5] Their charm makes them attractive, their power makes them hard to escape, but their impact on a culture makes them toxic. Durvasula contends that those who have a narcissistic style of behavior do not, and will not, significantly change.

Because their desire is control and power, their strategy is to knock down those over them or those who have the power they want. Their trademark mode of operation is verbal warfare and behind-the-scenes manipulation of others. They gossip, they argue, they question the skills of those presently leading, and they backstab and degrade and sealion (troll someone without desire to resolve the conflict) and scapegoat others.[6] Scapegoating results, sadly, in demonizing other people. The large number of criticisms Paul faced in Corinth has persuaded me that sealioning was being used against him by his opponents. Anything and everything he said or did was turned into criticism.

In many church and Christian contexts, the divisive band of people is marked by grandstanding, the desire to be recognized for virtue. Ironically, they often want this recognition through their own public affirming of their virtue. Furthermore, in the narrative of their own cause they often spiritualize their motives. ("We just want God's will to be done.") Or they may spiritually bypass their real emotions. ("I'm not envious of that person, I have a deeper spirituality than she does.") In all this, then, the divisive group works hard to make others think they are morally respectable.[7]

The Backstory: More Then Than Now

If we listen to Paul's words, we can attune our ears to hear his pain. We may find ourselves empathizing with him and perhaps even wanting to protect him from harm. The important thing is that we listen and remain open-minded to hear what he is saying.

I (Scot) know I never would have heard Paul's emotions and the allegations against him as well as I can now had I not learned from Adrienne's work in our cohort. With her understanding of how to help those who have experienced trauma in mind, I began applying her insights as I was studying Corinthians for my work on the Everyday Bible Studies series. I found that I was hearing more in Paul's words than I had ever heard before.

In one of my favorite novels, author Lil Copan observes that Paul "became the roaring voice of the early church."[8] He was that, but not always. Paul's roars sometimes cracked, creaked, and croaked, and in 2 Corinthians they become a whimper. We hear some weeping, along with clear signs of depression and despair. His Corinth-bound correspondence, if that is not too delicate a term for his at times white-hot missives, reveals a transparent, vulnerable, and deeply emotional man. One can't read the following lines from his back-and-forth with the unstable, and probably mercurial, house churches in Corinth without spinning one's head a bit to ask, Was Paul really that vulnerable with them? (Yes, he was.) Again, hearing Paul requires us to have ears attuned to and in empathy with him to hear the depths of what he is saying. When a caring pastor reads these lines on a Sunday morning, she may tear up, but such a pastor undoubtedly will reveal a tone of pained compassion. I have added italics to emphasize the words revealing Paul's sufferings and emotions. (If you still think Paul is a jerk, just read the words in italic font from *The Second Testament*.)[9]

> Up to the present hour we *hunger* and we *thirst* and are *shabby* and *slapped* and *destabilized*. (1 Cor. 4:11)

> For we don't want you to be uninformed, siblings, about our *trouble* that happened in Asia, because we were *depressed—excessively, beyond ability—so that we despaired even of living*. But we ourselves had among ourselves *the death sentence* so we might not be persuaded in ourselves but in God, the one who raises the dead ones, who rescued and will rescue us out of *such great deaths*, in whom we have hoped that he will also still rescue. (2 Cor. 1:8–9)

> For out of much *trouble and heart-anguish* I wrote through *many tears*, not so you may be pained but so you may know the *love* that I have *aboundingly* for you. . . . Coming into Troas for the

Christos-gospel and having a door opened for me in the Lord, *I did not have leisure in my spirit* in not finding Titos [Titus], my sibling, but, saying farewell to them, I exited to Makedonia [Macedonia]. (2 Cor. 2:4, 12–13)

In every way, [we are] ones being *troubled* but not
distressed;
ones *perplexed* but not overperplexed,
ones being *chased* but not abandoned,
ones being *tossed down* but not destroyed. (2 Cor. 4:8–9)

Make space for us! (2 Cor. 7:2)

Apart from the exceptions [to the above] [there is] my daily supervision, [that is], *the [inner] disturbance* for all the assemblies.
Who weakens and I don't *weaken*?
Who trips and I am not set on fire? (2 Cor. 11:28–29)

Picture that. Paul, an empathic, sympathetic, read-the-room's-feelings people-pleaser? It sure sounds like that to me. The Paul we meet here is not some stiff, stoical, sophisticated, tight-upper-lip bishop or rector who fulfilled his duties like clockwork. This is no jerk. This is someone who loved the Corinthians, though they at times refused to return the favor. He is homeless and without food, tested and often confronting possible martyrdom, and blubbering with "trouble and heart-anguish . . . many tears." His preaching voice is stoppered in his anxious waiting for good news from Corinth. He is all but begging for their reciprocal love. On top of this, he was a pastor overwhelmed by what needed to be done to accomplish his hopes for his least favorite church. Or perhaps they were his favorite but his most difficult.

I (Scot) love this Paul. I love him the way I love pastors I've known.

I respect them; I get irritated by them; I worry about them; I am blessed by them. Paul had formed enough churches at this point to have hundreds of children in the faith, evidently many of whom now considered themselves his supervisor. As odd as that may sound, it is no surprise to anyone who has led anything in a church. Church people have plenty of opinions about seemingly everything. What continues to fascinate me about Paul is his traveling back-and-forths from Ephesus and elsewhere to Corinth. Back-and-forths that were both in body and by letter, and at times he was represented in body by one of his close coworkers, such as Titus (2 Cor. 2:4, 12–13).

This emotionally, personally vulnerable Paul forms the personality of the backstory of Paul's testy relationship with the house churches in Corinth. Most of us know Christians, even some church leaders, who think with their feelings and feel with their thoughts. Such persons are not just intuitive, they are in touch with themselves. Paul's second letter to the Corinthians, unlike any document from the earliest churches, reveals an in-touch Paul who, sad to say, has been overinterpreted and weaponized by too many who are themselves out of touch with themselves.

The Backstory's Details

Only specialists of 2 Corinthians enjoy getting lost in the intricacies of the back-and-forths of Paul and Corinth. It's so complicated that many just give up. Others (and I understand their views) don't care about reconstructing the back-and-forths because they just want to read the letters. So in what follows I hope to provide a basic sketch of what is happening—the backstory behind the letters as best we can tell.[10]

A woman named Chloe has asked Paul a fistful of questions. In doing so, she or some others at the church have dished out some scoop about people and problems in the church of Corinth (1 Cor. 1:11–12). At the end of Paul's first letter we learn that three men were probably the scoopers (Stephanas, Fortunatus, Achaicus; 16:17). That letter and their trip were only the beginning of a series of trips and letters between Paul and Corinth. Listening to Paul's own words about what others were saying and what he said back is a bit like driving a car with no windows. Paul is a courageous letter writer, but by his own admission not so courageous in person. Whether he was showing off his courage or sitting in a corner, the man clearly loved the Corinthians and longed for restoration with them. He also yearned for them to get their act together.

We know Paul wrote a number of letters to Corinth. Two have survived in our New Testament. There were also letters written from Corinth to Paul, though none of these have survived, except in bits of quotation found in the two surviving letters of Paul that we have. Many today have concluded that our second letter to the Corinthians combines two or more letters of Paul into one. Here's a brief outline of how at least five letters were written and delivered, based on one of the most informed sketches of the backstory made by a lifelong specialist on Paul.[11]

Paul was in Corinth several times. He founded the church and remained there for eighteen months (Acts 18:1–8). He returned about three years later (AD 55) in what is called the "painful visit" (2 Cor. 2:1; 12:21; 13:2). After writing 2 Corinthians, Paul arrived again in Corinth (Acts 20:2–4). During this time, five letters were written between Corinth and Paul.

Letter A: *by Paul* from Ephesus, mentioned in 1 Corinthians 5:9, but which we probably do not have. Some think letter A could be reflected or cited in 2 Corinthians 6:14–7:1.

Letter B: *from Chloe's household* about Corinth. This letter details divisions among believers in Corinth (1 Cor. 1:11).

Letter C: 1 Corinthians *by Paul* from Ephesus, which responds to the issues bobbing up and down in both letters A and B and more. Taken to Corinth by Timothy (or perhaps others). Timothy returned to Paul in Ephesus (1 Cor. 16:12).

Letter D: *by Paul*, the "severe" letter (2 Cor. 2:4; 7:8), which is at least reflected in 2 Corinthians 10–13. Titus delivered the letter. Paul requests Titus to meet up with him in Troas (north of Ephesus).

Letter E: *by Paul*, our 2 Corinthians, from Macedonia. Titus, with others, delivered the letter to the Corinthians.

On top of this, Paul sent Timothy and Titus to Corinth to mediate the tensions (1 Cor. 4:17; 16:10; 2 Cor. 2:4; 7:8). Most of what happened between Paul and the Corinthians, other than the eighteen-month founding visit, occurred from Paul's mission hub, Ephesus, through letters and Paul's envoys. In the middle of it all, Paul was attacked by congregants in Corinth and perhaps, too, some outsiders who showed up and caused disturbances over Paul's leadership (2 Cor. 2:5–11; 7:8–13). Even after one apparent resolution to the tensions, another disturbance occurred (2 Cor. 10:10; 11:27; 12:6–7). And let's be honest: This simplified sketch involves complications that are far from easy to settle. What we can all agree on is that Paul and his children in the faith in Corinth were more often than not at odds with one another.

Paul had one advantage, if I can call it that, and it permits us to identify with him in ways we cannot identify with other church leaders or pastors. Paul was not a local pastor in Corinth dealing with his parishioners. He was an apostle on the move who resided for much of the time during which this conflict occurred—months and minimally weeks at a time—away in Ephesus. Paul's disadvantage was that he was not local, residing there at the church. Had he been there, he may have been able to settle some of these tensions directly, in person. On the other hand, perhaps, had he been there, the whole situation would have become untenable for his leadership.

Paul was more than just a church-planting apostle who zoomed in and then zoomed out. He loved the Corinthians, but he was a scorned lover in his relationship with Corinth. He likely had had a honeymoon start when he founded the church and stayed on for more than a year. But their relationship eventually deteriorated, and following that dustup he was anything but warmly received, respected, honored, and praised. He was the talk of the church gatherings. "Can you believe Paul told us to do that!" He was gossiped about. "Paul's arrogant. Pushy. He's not one of us." They degraded him. "The man has no idea how to organize an oration." A specialist on 2 Corinthians, Paul Barnett, sums this up by saying that the Corinthians "didn't trust his *sincerity*. They questioned his *adequacy*. They doubted his *integrity*. They didn't acknowledge his *authority*."[12] A female pastor who knows the ups and downs of the pastoral life, Barbara Brown Taylor, once observed in a sermon, with a wry reminder, the wider reality of the relationship of Paul and the Corinthians: "Everywhere he went he offended people, they said (which they, presumably, did not)."[13]

The Corinthians were no doubt offended by Paul. However, they did not seem to consider, as Taylor observed, how much they might have offended, wounded, and traumatized him. Plenty of us know what it means not to be taken seriously in our wounds and trauma. Many of us know the experience of being dismissed. Over time Paul had heard enough of what the Corinthians were saying about him that he pulled out every criticism he had heard and responded to it—while claiming he was not defending himself![14] Just what did the Corinthians have against him? What they had against him mirrors what many church folks have against many churches and Christian institutions. Those who say what they think often wound others deeply, and as a result many Christians have learned that their "calling," truth be told, is simply to absorb the criticisms and play nice. Paul must have missed that lecture, because he had some juicy words for the Corinthians. Here is where we find the authentic Paul.

Some More Backstory Today

When we attune our ears to Paul's backstory with the Corinthians, we have a thicker understanding of what happens in those tense, even harsh, moments in 2 Corinthians. And the same applies today. If we hear something that sounds a bit harsh from someone, we might be wise to ask questions such as

- What might be the backstory here?
- Is he learning to do things in a way that was not part of his previous experience?
- Is she learning how to lead?
- Is he having problems with his children?
- Is her family struggling financially?
- What have been her past relations with others?
- What happened in her past that might illuminate why she was so abrupt with that person's challenging question?
- Will we tolerate an emotional leader who knows her feelings, who communicates her feelings, and who thinks with her emotions and feels with her mind?

Another dimension complicating a backstory, especially when we experience anger from someone we are caring for, is transference. Transference can happen when a client transfers his feelings (anger, love, and so on) from another person to his therapist. But transference can also occur when a person, say a husband whose wife had an affair, transfers his anger at his wife from his wife to his pastor. Instead of expressing anger or outrage at his wife, he moderates his feelings toward his wife and transfers his anger to the pastor. This is even easier to recognize when the man's pastor is a woman. One time, when I was teaching undergraduates, a male student came into my office to talk. After a few minutes, he grew irritated, leading to expressions of anger toward me. My wife, who is a psychologist, and I had recently had a conversation about transference and, in a stroke of luck (which the student thought was genius), I began to ask him about his church and pastor. Not long into the conversation, he backed off his feelings of anger toward me and began to get angry about his pastor instead. I learned that one of the real causes of his anger was that pastor's lack of care for him when his older sibling was traumatized by a male authority figure.

When someone expresses anger toward you, you might learn to ask these kinds of questions: Do I know anyone this person might be angry with? Could I be an object of transfer? Does the emotion that I am receiving from them not seem to match the situation we are in or experiencing? You probably should not ask the person, "Hey, are you transferring anger to me from someone else?" Instead, try to sensitively probe in a few directions without being too direct.

Let's return to Paul. In the next chapter, we'll listen to him talking about the allegations the Corinthians have sent to his inbox.

Chapter 5

Listening to Allegations

Leading people invites feedback, which can be both positive and negative. Welcome to leading! To invite feedback leads to suggestions, criticisms, allegations, and even accusations. Those who are open to feedback will receive more than those who are not open. And we also have to realize that some people in churches are just plain nutty. Leaving the general nuttiness aside, if we were to sit down over coffee with any leader, especially one who is vulnerable and open, it's highly likely she or he has a story or two to tell of criticisms someone has recently brought to their attention. Not long ago, Kris and I were leaving a church when an elderly lady pressed her concern on the pastor. Evidently someone had left out some tables the night before. The concerned lady and her husband had seen them later in the evening. "It's not right," she said to her pastor. "What happened?" All the pastor knew was "someone took care of the tables this morning before the service." The elderly lady just shook her head. Small potatoes, to be sure, but pastors are the ones to whom congregants take their small taters, and what is a small tater to some is a big potato for others.

Pushback, whether large or small, is all too common. Some will target competence; others aim at your character. Competence and character, those are the two big ones. Keep these in mind as we proceed through the allegations and accusations the Corinthians made about Paul as they "left Sunday morning's service." And keep this in mind about congregants and congregations: "One of the most time-consuming things is to have an enemy."[1] Those words unmask what happens in churches when a person or a group decides someone is their opponent, and even an enemy. The decision to make someone an opponent can infect a group, and infections expand. Expanded infections become obsessions, consuming large amounts of time.

A friend involved in a school dustup recently wrote me about how much time it took to come to an agreement on what looked to him to be small taters: "Through a series of meetings that involved hours and weeks of my time." Ask any leader who has ever become the enemy and their story will be filled with meetings and false starts and turnarounds and abrupt changes and more meetings.

A Person's Trauma Is the Spouse's Trauma

Though the word *enemy* does not appear in the following story, the word *trauma* does, and as you will see it spread from the pastor to his wife, to self-doubt, to therapy, and eventually to his resignation. When someone becomes an opponent, all those connected to the opponent become opponents too. Infections spread.

> The streetlight glared pale through my window; I couldn't sleep. I looked at the clock: 2:30 a.m. How could my heart be racing?

Groping for my neck, I took my pulse: 110 beats per minute. My wife rolled over and whispered, "You okay?" I responded, "Yeah." We both knew I was lying.

My mind could not stop. How did I end up here? What did I do wrong? How could my church hate me this much? I performed the pastoral math: I officiated weddings. I attended funerals. I volunteered with kids' ministry. The church was growing. New staff was being hired. I did exactly what we agreed to in my job description. Yet days prior I was called into an unsanctioned, electronic church meeting convened by a board that had no purview over the senior pastor. Anxious, I logged on. As the room populated, I found it full of people, the majority of whom were "special invites." These were the most prominent families in the church.

I had just entered my own trial.

Fight, flight, or freeze: I froze. Over the next two hours, they aired their grievances, often Christianizing their language for the sake of legitimacy. I didn't diminish my personal weaknesses, but they refused to understand them as anything other than moral deficiency, even going so far as to attack my wife's character.

In that meeting the world slowed to a crawl. Was this really happening? Matthew 7:4 played through my mind. Could they be right? In an instant, I replayed every interaction over the previous two years. I could not find anything to justify their accusations. Was there a log in my own eye that I could not see? Self-doubt set in. Perhaps I was the person they said I was. Was the church worse because of me? I did the spiritual calculus again: Church attendance was up; discipleship was growing; worship seemed more spirited; the budget was growing; I was giving my time sacrificially; I openly loved this church. Could they not see it? Why would they treat my family with such disdain? I was certain there had to be a reasonable explanation. What did I do wrong?

I stopped that thought process. Only five minutes had passed. It was 2:45 a.m. My mind stopped replaying the past and turned toward the future. Hypervigilance must be the only way toward stability. I began to calculate every possible scenario. I assumed that if I could control all the variables, then they would stop attacking me. I played it out: "If they say this, then I'll respond like that. If someone attacks my wife's character, this is how I'll emotionally calm myself and respond with gentleness."

My wife looked at me again. "Are you alright?" My blank stare was all the answer she needed. My body felt ill. How could emotional anxiety have such dramatic effects in my body? Sleep was a stranger; I was on autopilot.

A few days later I received a text: "Check your email." One of the most respected leaders had sent a public email to the entire church defaming my character and my pastoral competency. He even placed my wife in his crosshairs. Reply All can be cruel; people began to pile on. Time seemed to stop; I froze again, lost in my own thoughts. How can I lovingly pastor this church? I checked my pulse; my heart was racing, but it couldn't keep pace with my mind: Where did I go wrong? What did I do? Why can't I make sense of this?

At my breaking point, I went to the chair of my elders board for support. I did my best to explain. My wife was in tears every Sunday morning. She dreaded going to church, but she feared being judged for not going to church even more. I was having panic attacks. I needed space. So I asked for a month off to seek therapy with my family. He agreed, so long as I promised to return every Sunday morning to deliver the sermon. He didn't want church leadership to show signs of weakness. Not knowing how to respond, I agreed.

Finally, we got a reprieve. With little energy left to sustain my facade, the depth of my exhaustion and woundedness was laid bare in therapy. My mind still couldn't comprehend how I got here. Where did I go wrong? The past held no answers, and the future was murky with fear. Should I even be a pastor?

Reluctantly I came to realize that my pastoral heart and my financial needs were being leveraged against me. Pastors don't always hold power in a church. My church held extraordinary leverage over me: They validated my pastoral calling; they set my salary; they owned my home; they were the dominant share of my family's social network. When church turned bad, no wonder I was overcome with the need to control every possible scenario and prevent their next attack.

It was here that my therapist told me that my mental process mirrored that of an abused spouse. I placed responsibility on myself for the free choices that someone else was making to attack me. The house would never be clean enough. The meals would never be good enough. The children would never be well behaved enough. No amount of perfection would ever be enough, and so the blows kept on coming. Was it really not my fault?

After several months of therapy and prayer, I built the courage to resign. My biggest fear still was disappointing them. Their critiques had a lasting effect. Perhaps I wasn't strong enough or spiritual enough to be a pastor. Discerning the spirits is a gift for a reason. I never saw the ways in which my honest affection for the church could be used against me. I never saw my propensity toward self-blame. I never saw my need for friends who could see from the outside what I could not see from the inside. I could not guard my heart by myself, and I am grateful for all those who walked with me and helped me fight the battles I could not fight on my own.

On the other side, I am still recovering. And I can graciously accept that though I will never be a perfect pastor, yet in his mercy Jesus has qualified me. I am grateful to Christ for sustaining my family and my vocational call to serve his church. I am an emblem of Jesus' body, which is capable of deep goodness and redemption.

This is a story alleging weaknesses of competence and character. This man and his wife were traumatized. I know them. They are good people. He's a good pastor. Being good, and even doing the right thing, does not prevent trauma. Church people can traumatize other church people.

What about Paul? Was he accused of character problems or of competency weaknesses? In what follows I (Scot) will briefly sort through the various accusations made by the congregants in Corinth against Paul. My experience teaching these chapters of Corinthians has taught me that most people read them and miss nearly all of the allegations against Paul. They are not listening—that's my response. Paul was blasted by the Corinthians. We would be wise to assume that Paul's closest friends were wounded when they saw Paul wounded. They, too, no doubt took some of the heat. The vulnerability we see in this letter reveals a wounded, traumatized apostle.

So let me give you two clues to look for in Paul's letter. First, that Paul was accused of incompetence and lack of character. And second, that Paul's responses were predictable. Once you see these things, you can't unsee them. Those who understand trauma will see it in Paul.

Paul Is Fickle

Whether or not Paul can explain himself, his critics in Corinth thought the man was fickle. Why? Because he altered his plans to visit them. Let's begin at 1 Corinthians 16:5–6, which we will call plan A. Paul wrote to the Corinthians, "I will come to you whenever I cross through Makedonia, for I am crossing through Makedonia, perhaps I will remain with you or even spend the winter, so you can send me ahead where I may journey." Don't you just love a plan that says "whenever" with a dash of "perhaps," then sprinkles a pinch of "where I may journey"? So plan A plots a possible trip from Ephesus to or through northern Greece's Macedonia, then south along the coast of Greece to Corinth, where he will wait for good travel weather and then be off to Jerusalem with his collection for the poor.

But apparently Paul reconsidered plan A and plotted, but again only plotted, plan B instead. In 2 Corinthians 1:16 he communicates plan B to the Corinthians: "I was deciding to come to you first so you might have double grace and through you to cross through into Makedonia, and again for Makedonia to come to you and to be sent ahead by you to Youdaia." This one is a bit more complicated to unpack. From Ephesus to Corinth, up to Macedonia, and then back to Corinth and then on to Jerusalem.

But again, instead of plan A or plan B, Paul actually traveled plan C, which mixes and matches A and B into an even more complicated road trip. From Ephesus to Corinth and then back to Ephesus, and then (like plan A) by foot north to Troas and then over to Macedonia, and then down to Corinth and off to Jerusalem. Truth be told, it looks like Paul even plotted a possible plan D, which he never made: Ephesus to Corinth to Ephesus and back to Corinth, and probably then back to Ephesus and then back to plan A, yada yada yada (2 Cor. 1:23).

Was Paul fickle? Even if these details are a bit too complicated for us to follow, the Corinthians thought he was. Their perceptions matter. Anyone who is questioned for being fickle, and who knows people are talking about him, will be wounded, one step closer to entering the trauma zone. I'm not sure how many readers of Paul listen to him with sufficient attunement to notice why he goes into such detail about his change of plans. He does this because their criticisms hurt him. That's why he sounds defensive.

There Are Two Pauls

Listen with empathy to how Paul characterizes himself in the opening verse of 2 Corinthians 10 (NIV): "I, Paul, who am 'timid' when face to face with you, but 'bold' toward you when away!" Reading carefully, we see that the allegation is that there are two Pauls, Mr. Timid and Mr. Bold. It just depends on whether Paul is face to face with someone. When he's perched in big-city Ephesus writing his letters, he's got big-city boldness. The Greek word translated as "timid" (NIV; *praütēs*) can also indicate impoverishment in a more economical sense. Or it could point to humility as a feature of his character. And neither self-impoverishment nor humility grew naturally on the branches of the Corinthian tree. Boldness, even brashness, was virtuous for them.

Here's another one: The Corinthians say his presence is "unimpressive" when he speaks, but his letters are the opposite: "weighty and forceful" (10:10 NIV). It was likely painful for Paul to be accused of being two-faced or speaking with a forked tongue. And that's why he raises this allegation first.

The accusation that Paul was timid and unimpressive is related to the manliness virtues of the classical world, virtues formed through success on the battlefield, oratory at the rostrum of the city, one's capacity to take a stand in leading a city, a victory on the athletic field, or the perfection of the body. Paul's models for conducting himself did not match the advice of their leadership manuals. Instead, Paul wanted to be formed to another image, that of the crucified, humble, and abused Lord Jesus Christ (1 Cor. 1:18–31; 11:1; Phil. 2:6–11). For Paul, being accused of lacking manliness was like an athlete being accused of being a sissy in a high-school locker room. They accused him of not having the guts to lead, of failing to take a stand when others were present, of not stating his view when others could refute it. Being called

Mr. Timid as a leader clearly wounded Paul the apostle. This is step two toward the trauma zone.

Paul Doesn't Look the Part

It's a proven reality that tall handsome people get hired sooner and move up the ranks faster. Attractive women experience the same benefits, though they experience more challenges moving up the ranks than men. Appearances matter, whether we will admit it or not. And sexism further confuses the appearance game we so often play. Second Corinthians 10:7 (NIV) reads, "You are judging by appearances." This sentence can be taken ironically, revealing to the Corinthians what they have not noticed, or it can be taken sarcastically, manifesting a touch of anger on Paul's part. A third option, which is even more likely after we take a quick look at Paul's use of "face" in verse 1, where it refers to his physical presence and appearance, is that Paul could be confronting the Corinthians for degrading him because of his unimpressive appearance. Essentially, they were telling him he didn't look the part.

The status-conscious Corinthians felt degraded to have someone who looked like Paul as their primary leader. Recent scholarship, utilizing the categories of impairment and disability, provides us with a much sharper profile of why the Corinthians may have been offended by Paul's body. And it begins by having the open-mindedness to ask, perhaps surprisingly to some, whether Paul was disabled. An exceptional new study by Isaac T. Soon[2] suggests that in Paul we can distinguish an impairment from a disability. (See sidebar "Impairment and Disability.") An impairment points to a person who does not measure up to the social ideal of a body. The label *disability* goes one step farther: The impairment prevents a person's functioning and capacity to move upward or about with freedom in society because of that impairment.

This leads us to ask, Was Paul impaired physically? And if he was physically impaired in not achieving the physical ideal for a male, was he also disabled? Did his impairment affect and limit his social status? The answers to these questions vary from the possible to the probable to a simple yes. But the preponderance of evidence is now reasonably clear. Yes, yes, and yes. Again, the recent study by Soon establishes that Paul (1) had a "thorn in the flesh" that he calls a "messenger of Satan" (2 Cor. 11:14; 12:7), which Isaac Soon suggests refers to a spiritual battle orchestrated by God to prevent Paul's speaking about what he heard and saw in the heavens. This was a divinely created impairment on the path to status among the Corinthians. He could have gained glory if he could have talked about what he saw.

Impairment and Disability

While an impairment is a condition that is functionally and or aesthetically deviant from a socially constructed bodily ideal, a disability is an impairment that generates negative effects in its social and cultural environment. As impairment depends on a socially constructed ideal, so too does disability rely on an environment-unfavorable reaction to an impairment.

—ISAAC T. SOON, *A DISABLED APOSTLE*, 9.

Paul may be able to speak of this heavenly, ecstatic, out-of-this-world experience in the third person, as he does in 2 Corinthians. Yet he somehow knows that the "messenger of Satan" will prevent him from giving details. It may help to imagine an imaginary conversation with Paul about this.

Paul: I have had extraordinary visions of what God has planned.

Interlocutor: What did you see?

Paul: I'd like to tell you, but God has blocked me from being able to give specifics by sending a bad angel into my life who prevents me from speaking about what I saw.

How do you think the Corinthians responded to the claim, "I have something special to say about this, but I can't tell you"? Not favorably.

Isaac Soon has a second indisputable impairment and disability for Paul: (2) That he was undoubtedly degraded and stigmatized physically in the Greco-Roman world because he was circumcised, which gentiles saw as an impairment of the ideal masculine form. Gentiles ridiculed and were disgusted by those who were circumcised. Because circumcision affected a Jewish man's capacity to enter society, circumcision was a disability.

The Corinthian Roman wannabes all knew Paul was circumcised because he made it abundantly clear by his behavior and talk that he was a Jew. Furthermore, if Paul had visited any local gymnasium or bathhouse, well, it would have been obvious that he was stained with an impairment that would have established a glass ceiling for his status.

Isaac Soon points to a third impairment and disability for Paul, one that is almost as undeniable, yet neglected by many Bible readers: (3) Paul was likely a very short man, which was yet another occasion for ridicule because he failed to measure up to the standard of the Roman masculine image, which is not that far from the standard of our world: tall, muscular, thin, handsome.

Before digging into this third impairment a little more extensively, it should be clear that I consider each of Soon's explanations likely, if not probable. The specifics of the allegations against Paul—that he did not look the part—meant that Paul did not belong on the platform or behind the pulpit, and he did not measure up to the stature of a manly man who could lead such a self-approving robust group of people in Corinth.

The category of not handsome, not impressive, or not appealing physically describes Paul's failure to live up to the ideal Greco-Roman image of the man fit to lead and act with social, if not divine, authority. So why does Soon believe Paul may have been short? Soon uses the technical definition and applies discussions today of dwarfism in discussing Paul. Yes, that's right. Consider that the average male height in Paul's time was approximately 5'4" to 5'6" (64" to 66") and the average weight was 130 to 145 pounds. The average male in the USA today is 5'9" (69") and the average weight is just shy of 200 pounds. So at the very least, Paul would be short in our world. A height of 5'4" today would make Paul statistically short by American standards—only 3.6 percent of American males. But we should not measure Paul's size according to American statistics. Males are far taller today than they were in Paul's time.

But let's also consider a few other data points. The Greek name Paulos means "small." Perhaps this may have been his nickname, especially in the Greco-Roman cities where he planted churches. Consider another example of Paul's resisting the Corinthians with a Christ-reshaped approach in responding to their allegations against him. Here is 2 Corinthians 11:30–33 (NIV) with my own emphases in italics: "If I must *boast*, I will boast of the things that show my *weakness*. The God and Father of the Lord Jesus, who is to be praised forever, knows that I am not lying." The apostle chooses to boast about his weaknesses, and that may well have included his lack of stature.

Isaac Soon's final, and perhaps best, example of Paul's weakness is this: "In Damascus the governor under King Aretas had the city of the Damascenes guarded in order to arrest me. But I was lowered *in a basket* from a window in the wall and slipped through his hands." I'll admit I've never been able to think of anything other than a picnic basket when I read this. How big was this basket? Don't think of it like the baskets in those massive hot air balloons. The Greek term in this quotation for basket is *saganē*, and the term in Acts 9:25 is *spuris*, a relatively small food basket. (There it is again: picnic basket!) Soon's study of these baskets concludes that the basket in which Paul was lowered could hold and contain the weight of only a very small man—at most approximately a shade or two above 100 pounds. Again, consider that the average male in Paul's world would have been somewhere around 135 pounds. If Paul is around 100 pounds, he's about three quarters of an average-sized male. And for Paul to fit into such a small basket, as the terms would suggest, he would need to be either very small, short, or severely underweight, even emaciated.

Here's a text I have long thought close to describing the apostle's body, and it is a second-century text called the *Acts of Thecla and Paul*. Here I am citing Soon's translation:[3]

> A certain man named Onesiphorus, hearing that Paul was coming to Iconium, went out with his children, Simmias and Zenon, and his wife, Lectra, in order to meet Paul. For Titus described to him of what sort Paul is with regard to image [what he looked like must have been noticeable]. For he had not seen him in the flesh but only in the spirit. And he travelled down the Royal Road to Lystra, and he stood anxiously and looked at those who were coming according to the information from Titus. Then he saw Paul coming, *a small man with regard to height*, bald on the head, *curved in the legs*, healthy, monobrowed, to a little degree, an aquiline nose, full of grace. Sometimes he appeared as a man, other times he had the face of an angel.

The author of this early Christian text appeals to Paul's weakness in stature to reflect the glory of the gospel ministry he exercised. In this text, Paul is called "a small man" or a "tiny man" (*anēr mikros*). If this "little" indicates his height, one might assume Paul was approximately 4'8", perhaps shorter, say, 4'6". In a world in which tall and handsome reflected a virtuous man, and short and bowlegged indicated a man without virtue, Paul had a heavy burden to overcome the moment his new audiences saw his body.

As best as we can tell, Paul's unattractiveness had to do with shortness, his bowleggedness (which could indicate dwarfism; *achondroplasia*: short arms, short legs, larger head, average trunk[4]), his common baldness, and his lack of physical presence. Paul lacked the typical physiognomy of a leader who could lead the higher-status individuals in Corinth. Even the earliest images we have of Paul emphasize his baldness, his beard, his bowleggedness, and, at times, his shortness. The artistic representations of Paul fail to render him with an image that fits the ideals of Rome and Greece. Isaac Soon summarizes it like this: "Persons with short stature and dwarfism were stereotyped, made the object of humour and derision, and subjected to violence and processes of dehumanization."[5] The messianic pretenders about whom Josephus tells us were, as stereotypes would expect, tall.[6]

Like so many today, the Corinthians wanted the man or woman on the platform to look the part. They wanted someone who was tall and handsome and beautiful. Those who are platformed on Sunday's services are often scrutinized for their appearance, both their looks and their clothing. This is especially true for women, who are judged for what they wear and how they appear. Jennifer Testa Hrynyk, a pastor, explains the process a female preacher goes through in choosing an outfit. Not a skirt, since she will need to sit down with the children during the children's sermons. Not leggings—they're too tight. Pants, but not too trendy. Shoes, not heels—they're too sexy. The top, she ponders, cannot be too form fitting, so "she chooses a top that's long enough to cover her backside." Hair, too, matters. Colors of her outfit matter too. When it comes to style, that matters too: not too casual. It was easier, she muses, when she wore a robe. Her conclusion: "As worship leaders, we need to make informed and intentional choices that reflect the function of our office as worship leader and are representative of our church, while honoring our personal identity and the image we wish to project about ourselves through our clothing."[7]

And while the previous generation's standard for a pastor to dress the part and thus to help look the part has fallen away for many today, people continue to judge the pastor by what the pastor wears and how the pastor looks. A wise pastor avoids a power struggle over appearance, and dresses at the level of, or slightly above, the expectations of the pastor's congregants.

Back to Paul. Criticism of his appearance was a major criticism of Paul, and surely was leveled often and deep enough for Paul to raise the issue in his catalog of criticisms he brings to the surface. If we read his words with listening ears and draw on our ability to empathize, we can feel the weight of shame Paul may have felt because he had a body that didn't match social expectations.

To this point we have looked at three direct accusations against Paul. One accusation can be deflected; two are harder to deflect; but three—with more to come—are nearly unbearable. Competence and character are the fundamental allegations the Corinthians have against Paul, and now they attack his appearance as well. Paul is likely by now, at least at times, in the trauma zone.

Paul Is a Mediocre Talent

Paul was caught in a web of allegations and refutations, which looks an awful lot like what we call gaslighting today, including the accusation that he amounted to nothing but a mediocre talent, at least in the Corinthians' world, in which you competed for honor. They knew how the competition went, and they judged the competition on the basis of well-known rhetorical skills. Rhetorical skills measured the man, and the Corinthians thought Paul had failed the quest to honor because he lacked sophistication and eloquence when he spoke.

In the first paragraph of chapter 10, Paul turns over an accusation by the Corinthians that he operated in worldly ways. Ralph Martin, another expert on 2 Corinthians, describes their allegations against Paul in these words: "Paul was no pneumatic person, singularly lacking in demonstrable, charismatic gifts of leadership."[8] Notice next Paul's own summary words: "For some say, 'His letters are weighty and forceful, but in person he is unimpressive and *his speaking amounts to nothing*'" (2 Cor. 10:10 NIV, emphasis added). Maybe we should recall here that when Paul was preaching in Troas, a young man named Eutychus fell asleep—perhaps because of a boring sermon—and fell to his death, only to be revived (Acts 20:7–12).

This criticism of Paul's apparent lack of speaking skills stabbed his heart, to the point that he brings it up again in the next chapter. If you listen with ears attuned to the man telling his story, you will see that this time he concedes some of their point: "Even if I am self-taught in word" (2 Cor. 11:6). Paul was what we call an autodidact: a self-taught person. This means he was not educated in the Roman-Greek style of rhetoric and never had any teachers in that style. This one seems to have bothered him. We know this because he said the same in his first letter to the Corinthians (1 Cor. 2:1–5). At the beginning of the last chapter of 2 Corinthians, Paul repeats this lack-of-skills accusation with yet another expression, responding back to the Corinthians with a barbed comment: "since you are demanding proof that Christ is speaking through me" (13:3 NIV). How piercing it must have been for him to be accused of not even being an agent of God, someone through whom Christ is *not* communicating! One could easily surmise there may have been some interrupting and guffawing when Paul was speaking. One would be just as accurate surmising that they preferred Apollos's presentations over Paul's speaking (1 Cor. 1:12; 3:5–15). Paul knew the rough side of the Corinthians' tongue when it came to his sermons and speeches. All of this had been festering and hurting Paul for more than five years. Nothing wounds a speaker, teacher, or preacher more than being told they're not good enough at the craft that makes or breaks them. Again, in all of this, Paul is traumatized.

Paul Doesn't Act the Part

The Corinthian world valued a leader's boasting, but only if done well and within proper limits. An important observer of Greek customs, Plutarch, even wrote an essay on this, calling it "On Praising Oneself Inoffensively." Jewish historian and, at least according to his own autobiographical comments, skilled military commander Josephus boasts about his credentials in a way that his Roman audience would have valued: "While still a boy, really, about fourteen years old, I used to be praised by everyone because I was book-loving: the chief priests and principal men of the city would often meet to understand the legal matters more precisely with my assistance."[9] Today, self-promotion like this rubs us the wrong way. It sounds arrogant. But in Paul's world, anyone with status would be required to document their deserving status with at least some measure of boasting. Paul refused. Not only did he refuse this form of boasting, he had a very strange form of boasting to replace it, according to the very-concerned-about-status Corinthians. We will get to that in just a moment with what we call "gospel fawning."

The Corinthians expected Paul to boast of his accomplishments, and Paul could have taken the bait, boasting of the growing house churches in Corinth and its surrounding villages (including Cenchrea), but instead he checked his boasting. In Paul's rather clipped prose, he writes that

> we will not "boast" to the point beyond the measure but consistent with the assigned area's measure—which God measured as a measure for us, to reach even as far as you. For "we did not overreach ourselves"—as though [we were] not [to be] reaching you, for we arrived as far as even you with the Christos-gospel, not "boasting" beyond the measure "in outsiders' labors," yet having hope . . . your allegiance's growing . . . to be magnified to excess [in gospel work] among you consistent with our assigned area, to gospel beyond you, not to "boast" in "an outsider's already-accomplished [work] assigned area." *The one boasting, let the person boast in Lord.* For [it's] not the one affirming self who is approved, but the one the Lord affirms. (2 Cor. 10:13–17)

Sheer honesty gives credit where credit is due. Paul refuses to take credit for the gospel successes of others. His boasting is chastened. What's worse is that he turns the whole world upside down because he boasts in his sufferings. He diminishes his status and boasts in his losses, defeats, sufferings, and humiliations (2 Cor. 11:16–12:10). You could even say Paul gaslights their allegations that he is not boastful enough by boasting about what they dislike the most! I'm certain this approach did not go over well.

Paul did not act the part of a genuine teacher, and if he couldn't act the part, the Corinthians believed he ought not to be teaching.

Paul Plays Favorites

There's nothing quite like the pride of swelled chests when a congregation becomes self-sufficient and can afford its own pastors, staff, employees, and, when needed, experts. Not to mention a mortgage on a new worship center. And, to top it all off, paying off the mortgage. The Corinthians gloried in their resources. They were ready to hire a resident theologian, an in-house paid Paul who could be ready on a whim to teach. Paul refused their offer, and the Corinthians, marching as they were up the ladder of honor and social standing, were stopped in their tracks. Paul shamed them by refusing their support.

Paul's descriptions of what occurred diverge from the Corinthians' descriptions. Some of the words they use pop up in Paul's letters. Notice the words in Paul's question, words taken directly from the honor-shame textbook: "Was it a sin for me to *lower myself* in order to *elevate* you by preaching the gospel of God to you free of charge?" (2 Cor. 11:7 NIV). The word translated "lower" touches on a financial, resource condition. It can be translated "impoverishing myself." Paul did not just lower himself, he put himself in a difficult financial situation. He would not take their funds. Then Paul uses their words, like *plundered*, to describe their perceptions of what he was doing: "I 'plundered' other assemblies, taking a fee, to serve you" (11:8).

Here's where it gets edgy. The Corinthians knew not only that Paul refused to go on their payroll but that he had accepted support from other churches. He did so because he believed those churches were healthier and self-sufficient.[10] But the story gets explicit on this point. The Corinthians watched some Macedonians arrive and, with the Corinthians suffering some shame, they observed the Macedonians hand over resources to Paul: "and, being present with you and lacking, I did not burden anyone. For the siblings, coming from Makedonia, amply replenished the matters I lacked and in every way I kept—and will keep myself—from being a load" (11:9). The jagged edge of the story comes next: The Corinthians accused Paul of not loving them. Paul divulges their accusation indirectly when he asks, "Why [did I not take funds from you]?" Was it "because I don't love you?" (11:11).

Paul no doubt heard someone among the Corinthians say this. When a "you don't love me!" comes from the adults you've led to the Lord and have prayed for and have expressed love for, the room goes silent, with everyone staring at you.

No matter how Paul explained it, the Corinthians were too shamed to accept his practical theology of financial support. Paul did not take funds from churches until they were spiritually healthy and financially stable. His policy was a good one for the Corinthians—until it didn't work in their favor and wounded their honor. Out of shame they struck back at Paul, saying that he played favorites with Macedonia (and surely Ephesus) and did not love them. This wounded Paul because he knew in his heart of hearts that he had both a very workable policy and that he also loved the Corinthians deeply. Echoes of his response pop up in this letter more often than their terms of accusation (cf. 2:4, 12–13; 7:2–16; 11:11).

Paul Is No Longer Special

Whether or not they were insiders, or outsiders who invaded his mission territory (as in Galatia), some strong voices in Corinth claimed they were, when it came to public speaking, every bit "equal" to Paul (11:12). Their claim, which the Corinthians passed on to Paul and which some there accepted, was that Paul had no special rights to the mission territory at and around Corinth. Those who made such a claim were boasting about their own mission work in Paul's back yard. We might assume they also made use of the term *apostle*, so Paul rebuts them by labeling them "false apostles," and sarcastically as "super-apostles" (11:13; 12:11).

Again, their claims wounded Paul deeply. Paul knew himself as both their father (1 Thess. 2:1; 1 Cor. 4:14–17; 2 Cor. 6:13; 12:14–15) and their mother (Gal. 4:19; 1 Thess. 2:7; 5:3; 1 Cor. 3:1–2).[11] Furthermore, he levels his relationship to them when he calls them siblings, or "brothers and sisters." Paul experienced the shift in their looking from himself to others for guidance and leadership as betrayal, as duplicitous, and as unfaithfulness. His love for them was not reciprocated, even as they accused him of not loving them! Fractures in churches nearly always get wonky, with false accusations and false narratives about the other. Many explanations have been given of those famous words that open 1 Corinthians, but the best explanation is that Corinth had formed into personality cults.[12] Whether or not those names—Paul, Apollos, Cephas (Peter), and "Christ"—were plastered on the house church's door to name the church, there were at least devotees of Paul, Apollos, and maybe too of Peter and others (1:10–17). For many at Corinth, Paul had become the no-longer-special founder. One reading of the first chapter of 1 Corinthians is that Peter was Paul's biggest rival preacher, but only if you don't count Apollos! Paul may have been judged the third best preacher of the lot.

It's hard to grade the depth of the wounds Paul had experienced, but this one had to have ranked among the deepest.

Summary

How would it feel to be accused by those you love deeply with one or more of the following accusations, simply because you sought to exercise the gift God had granted you? They say:

1. You are fickle.
2. You are two-faced.
3. You don't look the part.
4. You are a mediocre talent.

5. You don't act the part.
6. You play favorites.
7. You are no longer special.

Most people are deeply wounded by such criticisms. And truly, there is only one term that fits the experience of having those you love and trust turn against you in betrayal. That word is *traumatized*. Remember, trauma is the sense of being overwhelmed, and it leads to the typical responses of fight, flight, freeze, and fawn. Anyone would be traumatized if these accusations were to land in their inbox. Let's not pretend Paul was a Stoic. Just read 2 Corinthians straight through some evening. The man was uber-emotional.

The accusations leveled against Paul and his at times erratic responses in these letters to the Corinthians indicate Paul was traumatized. Recently, a former chaplain known for his work with seminary students to prepare them to care for the traumatized, Peter Yuichi Clark, experimentally diagnosed Paul's trauma as PTSD (post-traumatic stress disorder) on the basis of diagnostic criteria in the *Diagnostic and Statistical Manual of Mental Disorders–5*.[13] I'll summarize some of the more analytical language of the *DSM* as "diagnosed" by Clark, though some of this language comes directly from the *DSM*.

First, Paul had experienced a traumatic event, not least exposure to death.[14]

Second, intrusive symptoms are apparent in Paul, like distressing memories and recurrent exposure to cues that resemble the original traumatic event.

Further, Paul's self-described state indicates hypervigilance and a disturbance in his sleep patterns:[15] nights in which his sleep barely extended beyond dreams.

Clark goes about diagnosing a nearly two-thousand-year-old apostle with genuine humility and caution about what can and can't be said. Personally, I see no reason to lock down too tightly on this diagnosis, though it seems reasonably clear to admit that at the very least, Paul exhibits signs of trauma. If so, a diagnosis of PTSD may help explain that trauma with even finer nuance.

So how does it help us to see Paul as a traumatized apostle? What benefit is there for us in seeing him this way? Understanding Paul's backstory and his relationship to the Corinthian church not only helps us better understand the Bible, it also informs how we think about the church and how we treat one another as Christ followers. Because what the Corinthians needed—and what we need today—is not just a trauma-informed church but a trauma-sensitive one. To this point, we have emphasized the skill of listening to Paul carefully, and that skill leads us to a more trauma-informed and trauma-sensitive approach to reading Paul. But we're only partly to our destination. We must proceed further and look at the identifying marks, the pillars, that support a healthy trauma-sensitive culture or environment. We believe there are six pillars offering this support, and in part 3 of this book, we will look at those six pillars in more detail.

Before we get there, however, we have more to learn from Paul as we deepen our listening skills even further to hear the pain in Paul's responses to his critics in Corinth.

Chapter 6

Listening to Explanations 1

Responses to Fickle, Appearance, Two-Faced

The foundation for the six pillars that form a trauma-safe space is the art of listening. The culture that underlies American evangelicalism is a talking, preaching, and teaching culture. But there is a time to talk, and there is a time to listen.

Evangelicalism is far better at the former than the latter. Talking often works effectively only after we've spent time listening. As a reminder, the five skills of listening are attunement, empathy, open-mindedness, protection, and deep breathing. And when I began utilizing these skills to listen to Paul, I discovered not only that he was in the trauma zone but that his responses to his critics—sometimes sharp and then at other times warm and gentle—match how people in the trauma zone respond. Recall again the major ways the traumatized respond: fight, flight, freeze, and fawn.

Fighting, more often than not, leads to a power struggle a person cannot win. Remaining under the powers in charge may well lead to what is called "learned helplessness." Learned helplessness is another form of fawning: capitulating to the powers to avoid the nastiness of defense, counterarguments, and conflict. We see this response at times when people leave a job without an exit interview or when a family walks away from a church simply by no longer showing up. In such cases it is often safer to disappear than to face an interview or engage in conversations that can lead to even more wounds for the person exiting. Those who leave churches and decide to discuss the reasons why with appointed leaders may well experience defensiveness from those leaders, further reinforcing their decision to leave. Exit interviews, even those done with the best of intentions and under the safest possible conditions, can sometimes rewound a person in the trauma zone. In some cases, what was revealed in the exit interview leaks out and becomes fodder for criticism. Eventually, the one who endured the exit interview will learn about the leaks, leading to yet more pain. Sometimes people just have to leave.

Flight for Safety

Another response to trauma is a hyperarousal response: flight. This occurs when a person senses she is in such danger that the only way to secure safety is to get out of harm's way. Of course, flight can be emotional and psychological as well as physical and spatial. We see some evidence of flight in Paul. Some are inclined to think Paul simply traveled on from Corinth, but another possibility is to see Paul's response as flight. It is reasonable to think Paul protected himself from the threat of more abuse by fleeing the presence of the Corinthians. They probably saw him as a coward, and this partly explains why they called him timid. He feared their pushbacks, the weight of their counterpunches, and chose safety in Ephesus. I know I'm filling in some gaps in what is found in these letters, but the gaps are real: Paul left Corinth for Ephesus, his "favorite" church and his safe place, and he sent others to Corinth on his behalf. That explanation is reasonable.

Let's look at some of the specific indicators of flight in Paul, because what Paul did can also provide an example for many who would rather respond "by letter" than go face to face with those in power. Remember that staying safe and protecting oneself is a component of flight. Since Corinth was an unsafe environment for Paul, he returned to Ephesus. Thus, letter A, mentioned in 1 Corinthians 5:9, which deals with sexual immorality among the Corinthian believers, was sent from Ephesus. This means that from his flighted safety in Ephesus, Paul sent someone else both to transport the letter and to read it to the appropriate persons. Letter C follows a similar script to letter A: Timothy took the letter to Corinth, with Paul remaining in Ephesus. Timothy was Paul's representative (1 Cor. 4:17). At the end of 1 Corinthians, Paul stands with Timothy as together they face the criticisms against Paul. Notice how Paul's words are freighted with his embodied memory of his trauma, words that now come to the surface to guide and inform the Corinthians' response to Timothy: "Therefore, don't let someone devalue him" (16:10–11). While Timothy was in Corinth, Paul was attacked yet again. Timothy shouldered that attack for Paul, but he was unable to satisfy the critics, so he returned to Paul in Ephesus (2 Cor. 2:5–11; 7:8–13).

From the safety following his flight, however, Paul fights back by sending Titus with what is called the Severe Letter (letter D). Paul then starts the trip back to Corinth by going north, but Paul does not meet up with Titus until he gets into northern Greece, in Macedonia, where Titus arrives and passes on good news about the Corinthians. Evidently, despite all that has happened, they still like him. Paul's massive relief at hearing this reveals his emotional condition of anxiety

(2:13–14; 7:2–7). Still, Corinth being Corinth, Paul does not return to there (1) until after he, perhaps, got some more bad news out of Corinth and (2) until he had sent 2 Corinthians (letter E) to Corinth while on mission in Macedonia. Titus was his representative with letter E too.

I realize this sequence of events can be somewhat confusing. What matters is noticing that more than once Paul sent one or more of his most trusted coworkers, Titus or Timothy, to travel back to Corinth to deal with Paul's accusers and their many allegations about his weaknesses. These representatives no doubt endured heat for Paul when they delivered the letter, heard responses, responded to the responses, and then returned to Paul, where they could safely discuss what was happening with the Corinthian church and how to respond. I know that today many people believe it is best simply to get together in a room and hash it out. While that can work for some personality types, it does not work well for others. Noncontrarian introverts want no part of hashing-it-out sessions, and most of the time such persons will simply fawn to get out of the situation. Others have learned that time and distance provide healing and perspective and that there will be opportunity for a later, more redemptive conversation.

The apostle Paul must also have believed that both Timothy and Titus stood a better chance at resolving the issues in Corinth, perhaps because the church was not attacking Timothy or Titus. Instead, they were indirectly attacking Paul's sense of his own character and competence. So Paul sought shelter in distance while those colleagues pastored these troubling situations for him.

Paul's motives were certainly more complex than any one theory can explain. However, we must consider trauma as a resource for explaining Paul's distance from Corinth. Distance did not lead Paul simply to forget the Corinthians. While in Ephesus and separated by the Aegean as well as a long trip by foot or by boat or both, Paul still seems to have been consumed by the problems raging in Corinth. He likely experienced insomnia and other symptoms of stress, anxiety, depression, and trauma. According to modern trauma theory, Paul could have been experiencing hypervigilance in his fixation on the situation at Corinth.

Whether or not you agree that Paul was showing a flight response to trauma, we all need to see his humanity more completely. Paul chose to flee Corinth, and he left for Ephesus—most likely because it was safer for him. Like any of us, Paul needed that safety to clear his mind and write a more balanced letter, but he wasn't passive. At a distance, Paul fought back. Let's take a closer look at how he did that.

Fighting Back as a Strategy for Finding Safety

Don't be surprised if someone you know who is in the trauma zone fights back. In fact, expect some amount of fighting back, especially by those with authority, leadership, and a confident personality. Fighting back is one of the body's responses when it perceives it (the whole person) is in some kind of danger, whether physical, emotional, psychological, or sexual. Fighting is one way a body seeks to secure its safety. We should not immediately connect fighting to a personality disorder or to being belligerent. This needs discernment, not dismissal. If our goal is to nurture trauma-safe and trauma-healthy communities, then we will learn to recognize fighting back as a legitimate response to trauma.

Remember, Paul was accused of being fickle and two-faced, that he didn't look the part, that his skills were mediocre, that he didn't act like a robust leader, that he played favorites, and, to top the allegations off, that he wasn't anything special to the Corinthians. Most of us would crumble if people with authority or power over us said such things to us. This is especially true if we thought they loved us or if we have given much of our hearts to them. Paul's flights from Corinth empowered him to turn to fight mode and respond to each allegation.

The intensity of his responses (at least when read in the Greek) indicate just how deeply these allegations got under his skin.[1]

Responding to a Change of Plans

Was Paul fickle or was he just being flexible? Therapists know that people in the trauma zone often have explanations for what has happened, and is happening, to them. Their responses to their trauma are revealing, and their explanations often clash with the explanations of others.

So how do you think Paul would have responded if we asked him, "Are you fickle?" He likely would say, "I am flexible in the Spirit." Paul would not have owned being fickle. For example, rather than say he changed his mind at one point, he tells us that he surrendered his travel plans to the Spirit. Now, some people, likely because it is prescribed by their DNA, are planners. Planners expect others to stick to their announced plans. But Paul flexes in his planning; this flexible approach to planning shows up in 1 Corinthians 16:5–7, indicated by words like "whenever" and "perhaps" and "or even" and "where I may journey" and "I hope to remain for some time with you," all topped off with "if the Lord permits." Let's read that full passage with the words I just highlighted italicized: "*After* I go through Macedonia, I will come to you—for I will be going through Macedonia. *Perhaps* I will stay with you *for a while, or even spend the winter,* so that you can help me on my journey, *wherever I go.* For I do not want to see you now and make only a passing visit; *I hope* to spend some time with you, *if the Lord permits*" (NIV).

If you have the planning gene, you are probably rolling your eyes and may need a chair because you are feeling lightheaded. Paul's flexibility here reminds me of a time when I was reading the letters of Willa Cather. She wrote to her brother, Roscoe, with the same indefiniteness and open-endedness of Paul. Here were her "plans": "I hope I can go up to Lander on our return trip. Eventually I shall get to Red Cloud. I hope I can get mother to go to Denver for two weeks, as Elsie writes that she's not at all well. . . . Perhaps I shall stay at home until the late fall."[2]

Keep in mind that on the same day she had also written to her other brother, Douglass, "Perhaps we may take another driving trip among the Rio Grande pueblos about Española, if Edith is well enough. . . . After she leaves me I may go to Lander. Eventually I will reach Red Cloud, and then I hope I can persuade mother to go to Denver for a couple weeks. . . . I want to stay at home for a month or two, if it is agreeable to everybody, but I won't stay after I begin to get on anybody's nerves."[3]

Willa Cather's plans clearly were not firm plans but possibilities. The same is true with Paul. Clearly, detailed plans were not as important to him as the Spirit's guidance. So Paul firmly rejects the accusation that he is being fickle; rather, he is open to the leading of the Spirit. In response, he fights back.

Paul begins by exploring his conscience, his inner world, and his motivations. He counters that his conscience is clear—as far as he can tell—and he believes his conduct toward the Corinthians is done with Christian character. When Paul looks inside he finds "transparency" (2 Cor. 1:12). And in 1:15 he writes that he is persuaded of his self-perception. He did not operate with "fleshy wisdom" (1:12; 1:17) but acted "with God's grace." Second Corinthians confirms 1 Corinthians, indicating that the content of his letters is not fickle (1 Cor. 1:13). Flipping the conversation from allegations to defense of his actions, Paul argues that there ought to be mutual congratulations, some co-boasting: the Corinthians in him, and he in them (2 Cor. 1:14). Paul is convinced of his integrity, noting that he has visited the Corinthians twice (1:15–16). He believes that the accusation that he is fickle falls flat. Rarely do we find anything in the Bible that comes close to this kind of self-reflection on one's motive.

The accusation of fickleness claims that Paul's yes is not a yes but a no, and his no is not a no but a yes (1:17). In response, Paul shifts gears, speed, and lanes at the same time—all without looking in the mirrors. He shifts from his necessary travel plan adaptations to the utter consistency of his *logos*, his "word" or his theological message (1:18). Here we can add a tinge of criticism of Paul's logic: Consistency of his message does not mean his plans are consistent and therefore trustworthy. But Paul can't be bothered by that nuance, so he moves over into a new lane. A lane where what happens to the gospel is more important than his own plans. Paul argues that he adjusted his plans, a yes becoming a no, according to the gospel mission's needs.

Paul grounds his first-things-first plans and gospel message in God remaining allegiant to his promise. Paul's message has singularly and faithfully been about "God's Son" (1:19; cf. 1 Cor. 15:3–5). Adapting the yes-no language of the Corinthians, Paul says his message about Jesus is consistently yes. There is a consistent amen and yes in God's redemption in Jesus Christ, God's Son. Paul's words are gorgeous and memorable and profoundly Christ-centered words: "For as many as [there are] God's pledges, in him [they are] the Yes! Thus also, through him the Amen! is said to God for splendor through us" (1:20). God's yes evokes Paul's amen.[4]

Are we listening to Paul's explanation? Paul explains his flexible plans on the basis of God's promises being fulfilled in Jesus, and the order matters. God's promises in Jesus are first, and plans are second. The one who solidifies Paul's plans and message is God, and this same God solidifies the Corinthians. How so? This God "christened us" and "sealed us" and "gave the Spirit-pledge in our hearts" (1:21–22). Centering one's life on the gospel transcends and changes the course of a person's life and plans.

We can listen to and learn from Paul's decision to fight. Consider a committee meeting or group discussion where someone asks, "Why are we even here? What is our mission? What matters most?" Paul likely would respond, "We need to look at this specific decision in light of the gospel and our gospel mission." And that shift in focus can change everything. With the mission in view, previous discussions shift, new plans are formulated, and a clear direction is mapped. However, some may also be disturbed by a change of plans. Might we be more tolerant of those who adapt their plans if we know they are doing so at the direction of the Spirit and for the good of the gospel? One practical takeaway from Paul's example is that it might lead us—and those in the trauma zone—to ask ourselves how Christ- and gospel-centered our intentions and actions are.

Responding to Allegations About Being Two-Faced

By now it should be more than clear that the Corinthians didn't cotton to Paul's style of leadership. The Corinthians said that when Paul was present with them in Corinth, he lacked the necessary ingredients to lead: confidence, ego-strength, and manliness. He was personally timid and weak, if not shy and unassuming. He intentionally degraded his status in their presence. Thus, "I, Paul, who am 'timid' when face to face with you, but 'bold' toward you when away!" (2 Cor. 10:1 NIV). And he asked them, "Was it a sin for me to lower myself in order to elevate you by preaching the gospel of God to you free of charge?" (11:7 NIV). Paul lacked presence when he was present. Paul does all he can to explain himself, and those seeking a trauma-sensitive reading of Paul will want to listen carefully to what he wrote, to the intent behind it, and, when possible, to consider the emotions at play when he wrote his words.

I (Scot) have spent time with some of evangelicalism's most influential pastors and leaders. Once I was invited to a megachurch to speak at the weekend service and was taken to an impressive green room.

When the pastor entered, everyone knew he was there. He was not boisterous or loud, but his voice carried the room, his presence turned every face toward him in a kind of "[name omitted] is here," and his body communicated a powerful "I am somebody." He was regularly asked questions, and he responded, telling folks what to do. When I described him to Kris, I could recall the impression he made and still makes with me: He filled the room with his presence. Respect for him was obvious, and he knew it. When we had dinner with a team of leaders, he was the center of attention the entire time. There was nothing timid about his presence; on the contrary, there was a lot of the bold.

Yet another time I was invited to speak to a core group of Bible study leaders at a megachurch. There were about two hundred in this core group. Those who had invited me had picked me up at the hotel, and we drove to the church. When we arrived, apart from the usual hellos and how-are-you's from folks I was just meeting, I was taken to their green room. After a few minutes of chatting, one of the leaders informed me, "That's [name omitted]." Not sure who that was, I asked, "Who's [name omitted]?" Though I was in touch with two or three leaders at the church, I knew next to nothing about this world-famous pastor, though the mention of his name jogged my memory and I admitted I had heard of him.

The next time I spoke there, this pastor picked me up at the hotel, went to breakfast with me, and drove me to the church to make sure I got settled in. What I can say with assurance is that when he was in the room, he did not stand out. He was humble, courteous, gracious, and kind through and through. He had little presence, but it was combined with widespread, deep respect. In this pastor, I would say there was a hint of the timid.

Now, what would happen if this second pastor, flipping the switch when he was away, wrote back several severe letters to the leaders in his church? My guess is those leaders would experience a form of relational whiplash, something akin to what some of the Corinthians experienced with Paul. In his letter, we find Paul jumping through hoops to explain himself. A famous apologist once said to me (Scot), "Don't respond to your opponents. Win your audience." Don't let their accusations shape what you say; give the audience a better accounting and provide a better explanation. In his letter Paul tries to do both, and I believe that's one of the best indicators that he's writing out of distress and trauma.

The Corinthians said that Paul, when visiting the church in person, was much like that second pastor, and then was more like the first pastor I described when he was away in Ephesus or Macedonia. That's a serious allegation, as no one wants to be charged with being two-faced. Today, the accusation that a Christian leader is two-faced or speaks with a forked and flexible tongue amounts to an accusation of hypocrisy. They were saying to Paul, "If you can't be bold when you're in Corinth, don't go bold when you get to Ephesus!"

Some leaders flip and flop because they take the side of the person they talked to last. They are not able to make a decision on their own. Some really want others to make the decision instead of them, so they get someone else to utter the final word, and when pushback against the decision arrives, they blame the one they asked for help. It's clear the Corinthians thought Paul was two-faced—showing one face when he was with them and another face when he was writing a letter.

But again, Paul fought back. The emotions at work when someone fights back can vary from the cool and logical to the passionate and angry. Because he doesn't explicitly tell us how he feels—"Hey, Corinth, the next six words are white hot with anger"—we have to impute emotions to his words. What he does tell them is that when he arrived back in Corinth, he was going to put up his dukes. Here's how he puts it: "I beg you that when I come I may not have to be as bold as I expect to be toward some people who think that we live by the standards of this world" (10:2 NIV), and then at 10:6 he threatens them by saying that when he and his team arrive, they "will be ready to punish every act of disobedience" (NIV). Paul responds logically, coolly, and rationally in this context, deconstructing their words. They say he is worldly, so he counters, "If their accusation is true, then if they think carefully about it, he 'doesn't soldier consistent with the flesh'" (10:3). Flesh, in this context, is the flash of impressiveness and confidence. Paul lacks the power of a charismatic-gifted leader (10:2), so he defends his style of ministry: "I don't soldier along in a fleshy way and I don't manipulate you Corinthians with flashy, fleshy (rhetorical) weapons" (10:3–4). Fighting back further, he tells them he tears down status-shaped "reasonings" and "every high-status place raising itself against knowing God" and he captures "every mentality for Christos-obedience" (10:5 *Second Testament*). For Paul, fighting back is multifaceted. He warns that he can be his letter-writing personality when present (if he has to), then threatens that he will go to the mat with them, while countering their allegations with reasonable alternatives.

The fight gets even tougher, moving into nothing less than a face-revealing angry threat. Paul is fully prepared "to make right every disobedience" he knows in Corinth but will not act until their "obedience is filled out" (10:6). The NIV's stronger translation, with "punish" (I have "make right" in *The Second Testament*), features one element of the term Paul uses (*ekdikeō*), which points at an act that undoes what is wrong and then makes things right. Paul raises their allegations of being two-faced again in chapter 11. His letters may be bold, unlike his personal presence, but when he gets there, if things aren't in shape, he'll be bold in their presence too (10:10–11). Using their own words, Paul clarifies that when he was in Corinth, he intentionally impoverished himself or degraded (in their opinion) his status by refusing funds and resources (11:7). So he fights back again. This time by contending that he refused to be a "burden" or a "load" (11:9). He intensifies his fight by saying he is proud of his decision to minister to them free of charge. Paul ducks and dodges their criticism and comes back with his own counterarguments. Listening to Paul, it is crystal clear that he has been forced to defend himself. Listening to him also makes us aware that this is a man who has been deeply wounded by the charge that he lacks confidence.

When we are accused, most of us defend ourselves. A male whose social status and manliness (which was a Corinthian obsession) has been questioned will fight back. A traumatized person's body goes into hyperalertness, and they must choose whether to fight back or go into flight mode. The traumatized person's body determines the correct course of action for survival. Here Paul chooses to fight back.

I can envision Paul's readers putting some intensity into their picture of his facial expressions as they read the letter. The Corinthians would have heard some fightin' words in these six verses as they were read aloud. No doubt, the Corinthians were themselves put on the defense by Paul's fighting posture.

Responding to Criticisms of Our Appearance

Ask my wife, Kris. Or any of our children. Ask my students. Ask anyone, and they will all tell you I'm not a style mogul. Nor do I have the genes for style. I'd wear the same thing every day if I could get away with it. But I was not a little bit chuffed when my son loaned me his Pandas to wear to class one day. *Pandas* is the term the kewl kids use for a special pair of Air Jordans. Stylish they were, and one student said to me, "Scot, you went up on my style scale today." Truth be told, by the end of a full day of teaching in them, my feet were sore and my plantar fasciae were on fire. My lack of style, about which I can laugh without a care, reveals a much harsher reality that I have not endured—what women, including women leaders, endure constantly: inspection of their clothing and body, and allegations if they fall short of expectations.

I have not endured what Paul endured. Nor what Adrienne has endured. In June 2019, *Relevant* magazine published an online article titled "Watch Male Pastors Read Sexist Comments Female Pastors Have Actually Been Told." It included a video about seven minutes long. Here are just a few of the comments.[5]

- "During holy communion it's hard for me to concentrate when you said this is my body given for you; I think about your body and not Jesus' body."
- "When you walked in for the introductory visit, we thought you were the pastor's wife and we kept looking for the pastor."
- "Women shouldn't wear pants."
- "Don't you think that dress is a little too short?"
- "I keep picturing you naked under your robe."
- "I don't often say this to a minister, but you are really cute."
- "You better be careful eating so much; you don't want to lose that schoolgirl figure."

You'll notice that all of these comments are focused on the body and on the clothes worn to cover the female body. It should not come as a surprise that women's bodies are often critiqued. Not for being too tall or too short, or too flashy or too subtle, or too casual or too professional. Women are most often critiqued for being too female or not female enough. When it comes to how women's appearance is critiqued within the church, it is quite often a double standard. Women rarely critique a pastor or a sermon based on the man's appearance. It seems acceptable for men to have thoughts and comments on women's bodies, and it seems acceptable for men to share them. Not one of the comments read offered a critique on the woman's preaching style, her exegesis of the text, or her theological stances. I (Adrienne) am convinced that women, in our God-given bodies, cannot measure up to the expectations and standards of what many congregants think they need or want from us.

The intent of 2 Corinthians 10:7, is essentially this: "Look at things [me, my body] according to a face [and I'm not up to your expectations, am I!]" And 2 Corinthians 10:10 unveils the allegations made by the Corinthians, saying "his body's arrival [presence] is weak." These early Christian texts describing Paul's not very impressive appearance confirm that Paul's body could easily have been a challenge to the Corinthians. He was a little man. And little men get little respect in a manly culture.

Paul Transcends His Size

Paul evades their accusation by switching lanes into what gives him his self-esteem: his identity and calling in Christ. Maybe his critics were tall, muscular, and handsome and had a string of military or oratory ribbons decorating their tunics. In spite of their allegations, he concedes that they are Christians, writing, "If someone is persuaded in oneself to be 'of Christos.'" But Paul defends himself with that same identity in Christ: "just as one is 'of Christos' so also are we!" (10:7). The Lord called him and authorized him to carry on the gospel mission in Corinth, and he's not just a little proud of that. Still, he understands the Lord's rationale—it was "for your formation and not for demolition" (10:8). In Paul's arsenal for fighting back is his threat of arriving in Corinth and wielding a heavier than usual weapon (10:10–11). Paul may not look the part of a warrior, but he's not afraid to do what needs to be done.

Traumatized leaders who have been accused of not looking the part will inevitably experience comments about their appearance, direct accusations, and personal insults, and those may stick with them for a long time. In Cynthia Beach's wonderful novel about a megachurch pastor obsessed with looks, wealth, and his sexuality, the pastor's assistant, Trish, is expected to dress in a way that complements the pastor's style. When her pastor approaches her about her appearance, she wonders what is wrong with her, with her fashion choices, or with her nonfashion choices. But she also fights back—by beating the daylights out of her pastor in tennis! For her, that victory is more than a tennis accomplishment. It is her response to her pastor sexualizing her.[6] I'm not suggesting the Corinthians expected a sexualized body for their male leaders, but appearance and attractiveness are rarely set apart. What was clear was they did not think Paul looked the part of a Corinthian leader. Looks mattered to them.

Fighting for Your Own Safety Can Be Healing

Fighting back can put a person on the path to healing. Steve Carter's memoir details the loss of his dream job at Willow Creek Community Church, one of America's most (now in)famous megachurches, led as it had been by Bill Hybels. In the very middle of all the chaos, Steve walked away. He resigned. He took the side of the victims, and he paid for it. On his social media he read words like this from people he had known, loved, and pastored:

- "You are a coward."
- "You're a con man."
- "You're a disappointment!"
- "You do not deserve to be in ministry."
- "You bailed."
- "You're a joke."
- "I never liked you anyway!"
- "You abandoned us when we needed you most!"
- "You're what's wrong with the church!"

- "Shame on you, Steve Carter."
- "I hate you!"
- "You're a wolf in sheep's clothing!"
- "You're the worst &^£%+@¥ pastor ever!"[7]

Does it remind you at all of the allegations leveled against Paul? If responses like those Steve received (from those he loved, and whom he thought loved him) don't traumatize a leader—whether pastor or not, man or woman, young or old—nothing will. Steve's book records his journey through congregational abuse, betrayal, trauma, and the process of healing. How did he respond? Did he go all Paul and get angry? Steve was challenged in a healing context by a leader to come to terms with his anger, which led him to say these things in role-playing with a friend about his former pastor. In his writing, we are privileged to observe the fight in Steve:

- "How could you?"
- "You have ruined my life!"
- "You are disgusting!"
- "How could you ever harm those women, their families, and wreck their lives forever because you couldn't control yourself?"
- "You are the biggest narcissistic, selfish, ego-driven jerk and have no right to call yourself a pastor!"

Then he was asked to punch pillows. Steve continues,

> What did Bill take from me? My kids' faces flashed in my mind, and then Sarah's, their tears and sadness as we moved away from the home they'd known and loved. I let my fists fly. I could feel tears streaming down my face as things came up. My career. My congregation. My integrity. My confidence. My home. My friends. My

> dreams. My trust. My energy. My ambition. My security. My plans. My influence. My future. Everything stood still for several minutes as I punched, screamed, kicked, and ugly-cried through every question. Sweating and heaving, I slowly stopped and let myself stand very still. My mind was numb, and my heart was racing, but I felt calm. A peace washed over me that I hadn't felt since I learned of the accusations against Bill.[8]

God designed us to be angry at what we ought to be angry about.

As you read 2 Corinthians, you may notice that the tone of the last four chapters is dramatically different than previous chapters. Why is this? Perhaps, as he was writing, Paul got fresh news of an outbreak of criticisms, somewhere between chapters 9 and 10. That may well have occurred. But hearing fresh news doesn't fully explain the tone shift. The substance of the criticisms raised by Paul himself in these chapters has parallels in other parts of this letter and 1 Corinthians. The news may be fresh, but it is not all that new.

And yet the tone shift is so sudden and so volatile at times—sarcasm, defensiveness, irony, and lashing out drip from these chapters—that we should ask whether there is another explanation besides just hearing fresh news. Fresh news from Corinth would surely trigger Paul's former rejections again. So the intensity of the last chapters of 2 Corinthians requires a different explanation, I believe, and trauma best explains the tone.

Please keep in mind: Traumatized persons can strike back in ways that traumatize others. And just because someone dwells in a trauma zone doesn't mean they are innocent of all wrong. The tone, the harshness, the sarcasm, the irony, and the labels Paul uses in his letters to the Corinthians can be explained insightfully by trauma. However, being traumatized doesn't justify vehemency or labeling critics as evil and demonic. Ironically, Paul seems to be aware of what he's doing—lashing out, defending himself, flipping terms upside down—while doing his best to say he's not doing what they think he's doing. He knows what his critics are thinking. His emotions are visible and expressed. We have learned today that suppressing our anger can jeopardize our emotional well-being. However, becoming unhinged or lashing out at others jeopardizes our ability to lead, complicating relationships with others while traumatizing the targets of our anger. As we said earlier, church relationships can be exceedingly complicated and it requires skills to understand them, and one of the most important skills is listening well.

Chapter 7

Listening to Explanations 2

Talent, Status, Favoritism, and No Longer Special

I (Scot) am unaware of any sermon in American history spoken before American presidents that generated the kind of response that the Right Rev. Mariann Budde received when she addressed newly elected president Donald Trump at the National Cathedral on January 21, 2025. Kristin Kobes Du Mez helpfully summarizes a pointed and prophetic set of remarks the pastor made to the president himself:[1] "You've probably heard by now about the Right Rev. Mariann Budde's sermon on Tuesday. If so, you're probably familiar with her closing remarks where she addressed President Trump directly, asking him 'to have mercy upon the people in our country who are scared now'—LGBTQ children, undocumented immigrants, and refugees fleeing war zones and persecution."

The specifics of what she said, in that context and setting, are not our concern here. Instead, I'd like to focus on the responses, and again, Du Mez helpfully records several of them for us:

Immediately after the sermon, the president's response was rather understated: "Not too exciting, was it? I didn't think it was a good service, no. . . . They can do, they can do much better."

The response from MAGA loyalists, however, was scathing, in an utterly predictable way.

Republican Representative Mike Collins shared a clip of the sermon on X and wrote: "The person giving this sermon should be added to the deportation list."

Denny Burk, president of the Council for Biblical Manhood and Womanhood, called Budde "a false teacher who has no authority or right to speak in the name of Jesus," and added: "We don't need [the president] to be led away from Christ by an apostate priestess usurping the pastoral office."

According to Tony Perkins, Budde represented "the cause of America's decline": "What we heard today was not a prophetic voice from the church, but rather pathetic."

Speaker Mike Johnson alleged that Bishop Budde had "hijacked the National Prayer Service to promote her radical ideology," using the service "to sow division." All of it was "Shameful."

Charlie Kirk said Budde had wasted the honor she'd been given and the chance to unify the nation. "Instead, she disgraced herself with a lecture you'd hear on CNN or an episode of *The View*. What an embarrassment."

Joe Rigney of Doug Wilson's Christ Church and New Saint Andrews College got to the heart of the problem: "Women's ordination is a cancer that unleashes untethered empathy in the church (and spills over into society)."

Perhaps influenced by some of these responses, Trump upped his game, criticizing the "so-called Bishop," calling her a "Radical Left hard line Trump hater," and demanding an apology. "She brought her church into the World of politics in a very ungracious way. She was nasty in tone, and not compelling or smart." Also, the service was "boring and uninspiring."

The pastor's response to all of this? Gracious. "The contrast between Budde and the MAGA Christians is stark. In an interview with the *New York Times*, Budde made clear that she does not believe that she speaks directly for God: 'I'm saying, this is the best that I can do to understand and interpret what I believe our teachings and our scriptures and what the Holy Spirit might be wanting us to hear.'" Du Mez offered a brief commentary on this, saying,

> Budde holds progressive social views. That should come as no surprise to anyone familiar with the Episcopal Church or anyone who has read her work. But how does she hold those views, and how does she see her faith connected to her political convictions?
>
> In her own words (and in her actions), she makes this clear. She does not confuse her attempts to obey God with guaranteed victory. She is careful not to confuse her judgment with God's will. She attempts to honor the dignity of others, tell the truth, and remain humble, reminding all of us, herself included, that the line that runs between good and evil runs through every human heart—not between nations, political parties, or Christians and non-Christians.

Now, if you are the priest at the National Cathedral, and if you address words to the president in the mold of Nathan addressing David, you should expect pushback. Pushback can be unsettling and unnerving. Most of us, I daresay, would be afraid to speak our minds in such a public setting. Fear likely would lead us to remain silent and avoid severe pushback. So I thank God for this pastor's courage and words.

Paul, too, was the object of constant and penetrating pushback. All pastors and leaders live with some amount of pushback.

Enduring pushback can be excruciating, as some of the stories in this book illustrate—the pain, the angst, and the sleeplessness caused by the careless, reckless, damaging words and whispers of others. Some of those words may mean well, some can lead to change, while others are designed to damage and destroy.

Responding to Criticisms About Talent

Nothing wounds a pastor quite like being told his or her preaching skills are lacking or boring or over the heads of congregants. Some probably need to be told. If they are not, the evidence will be found in empty pews. The Corinthians evidently considered themselves expert judges of oratory. After all, the ancient world had no computers or tablets with which people could while their evenings away, nor did they have TVs for watching sports 24-7. Traveling speakers, like Dio Chrysostom, made their circuits, since one popular form of entertainment was listening to traveling orators.

Kris and I once spent a few weeks vacationing on the island of Rhodes. To anchor myself in that location, I read Dio's famous discourse *To the People of Rhodes*. What struck me was its length (as published). The English translation is more than eighty pages in the Loeb edition. That's a long speech. Slightly younger than Paul, Dio was a famous Greek orator who spoke on topics like virtues and philanthropy. His style was relaxed and fun, and he could hold an audience for hours. Speaking of some great men in Rhodes' past who pursued honor and climbed the status ladder, he said that "many in times past have even given up their lives just in order that they might get a statue and have their name announced by the herald or receive some other honor and leave to succeeding generations a fair name and remembrance of themselves."[2] Statues of the honorable decorated the streets of

Rhodes. In fact, there were so many statues that those newly designated as honorable, many of whom were great orators, were able to receive their own statue only by chopping off the head of an older statue and replacing it with the head of the recent honoree!

All of this is to say that Paul was being compared with orators like Dio, and Paul did not measure up. Paul exposed his (mediocre, to the Corinthians) skills when he publicly spoke in the forum of Corinth. That's where much of his public evangelism or preaching would have occurred, though he also would have used his workshop in the city's working district to talk about the gospel. But in those public places, Paul was vulnerable to comparison with the Dio types of the Roman traveling circuits. His skills did not match theirs, and the Corinthians were surely pleading with him to keep his speeches to the atrium-like, piazza-like, or table spaces of private homes. Hecklers likely graded Paul with verbal pushbacks, the equivalent of raising a placard with a three instead of a ten for his rhetorical skills. Do you know what it's like to speak after, or even before, someone you know everyone has come to hear? (I do, and my aim was always to get done and get off the platform.)

How did Paul respond? To hear his response we have to listen with attunement. He was traumatized by their insults. Their insults were personal, they were professional, and they were, Paul is quick to clarify, theologically off base. To begin with, Paul knows he can be bold and may well have to be bold when he arrives if the Corinthians don't change (2 Cor. 10:2). But 10:10 is the killer line that must have unnerved Paul: "his speaking amounts to nothing" (NIV). His *logos* did not deserve the status of an orator, so they degraded him for not measuring up. Fawning slightly, he admits as much when he writes, "Even if [I am] 'self-taught in word'" (11:6). In 1 Corinthians he had said the same: "I came not proclaiming God's secret to you with high-status word or wisdom" and his speaking was "not in wisdom's persuasive words" (1 Cor. 2:1, 4). The Corinthians, too, must have compared Paul unfavorably with Apollos (1 Cor. 1:12; 3:5–15). Paul's defense of not using the skills of the public orator, for at least some in Corinth, was lame, the feeble excuse of a country bumpkin. Or so the Corinthians thought.

Paul's slight fawning there now takes a back seat to his fighting. Regarding his lack of rhetorical boldness when present, Paul responds that he refuses to use the methods of the world and the flesh (2 Cor. 10:2–6). He pulls out the big stick by announcing that he will be bold if he has to when he gets to Corinth, and that his personal presence, if not his rhetoric, will match the heavy, harsh words of his letters (10:11). To the accusation that he is an autodidact and lacks the finesse of a trained orator, he simply switches lanes, claiming knowledge that comes from God and a power that comes from the Spirit, and that these two matter far more than oratorical skills (11:5–6; 1 Cor. 2:1–5). He claims Spirit empoweredness; they want verbal performance. I believe Paul knew his skills were not on par with the Dios of that world. So he chose to defend himself by claiming God's call on his life, the evidence of his churches, and the power of a gospel shaped by crucifixion instead of wordsmithing. He ditched their accusations. Yes, regardless of how he responded, we should still acknowledge: Their criticism hurt Paul.

We do not know how the Corinthians responded to his fighting words, though it is not hard to guess. We've heard it dozens of times in our own day. Some leaders and laypeople are accused of not knowing enough or, even more caustically, of not having a seminary education, of not knowing Greek (let alone Hebrew), and of not considering the most recent professional discussion. Many respond as Paul did:

- "I know Jesus."
- "The Spirit led me to say what I said."
- "I did my best."

- "I speak as God gives me words."
- "Look at the size of our congregation."
- "God has used me, I'm grateful, and I give him the glory."

Some of these defenses emerge from resentment, envy, jealousy, and even anger. But when it comes to loving, compassionate care for others, spirituality and impact often defeat sophistication and skill. What mattered to Paul was the reality of church after church he had planted from Syrian Antioch to Corinth. His undeniable and unimpeachable defense was "*you* are our letter, having been written in our hearts, having been known and read by all humans, manifesting that *you* are Christos's letter, served by us, having been written not with black ink but with God's living Spirit, not on stone tablets but fleshy, heart tablets" (2 Cor. 3:2–3, emphases added; cf. 1 Cor. 9:2). Paul believed he had defeated their "mediocre talent" accusation. But although he may have thought he defeated their accusation with his explanation, the criticism lingered in his emotions.

Responding to Criticisms About Status

As we've seen, boasting was not only acceptable for the Corinthians, it was expected—if done according to Roman and Greek form. The standard for boasting had been for decades the autobiographical brag sheet composed by Augustus in his famous inscription *Res Gestae Divi Augusti* ("things done by the divine Augustus"). Line after line recorded his accomplishments. The swelling of his chest (and head) are evident on every page. These accomplishments were engraved in public places throughout the Roman Empire.

Paul, however, did not noodle around when it came to boasting. He fought back, once again defending himself. He knew what he had accomplished and said so: the very existence of the Corinthian church, as well as several other church plants in Greece, all derived from his mission work. He refused to take credit for what his associates had done (2 Cor. 10:12–18). He had other punches to land. Paul refused to boast by way of comparison with others (10:12). He was glad if Peter and Apollos, not to mention Titus and Timothy, succeeded in their evangelistic and pastoral efforts. He once wrote to the Corinthians that "I planted, Apollōs gave to drink, but God was causing growth" (cf. 1 Cor. 3:6). Plus, he knew it was near idolatry and a mark of hubris to "commend himself." He knew God was the only one whose commendation was necessary (2 Cor. 10:18; 12:19).

With his underwhelming approach to boasting, Paul flips the script, turning boasting on its head. (Or at least he tries to.) His Christoform rhetoric leads him, ironically, to be braggadocious about his weaknesses and suffering. Starting at 11:1, and then developing his theme from 11:16 through 12:18, Paul presents the so-called Fool's Speech. Paul flips the term "boast" to exalt "foolishness" instead. He claims that what the Corinthians think are silly and low-status accomplishments are (paradoxically) the glorious work of the gospel of the one crucified. He fawns at the Corinthians' desire to claim high status, instead claiming low status as the only status that matters to him. It is possible, even likely, that the Corinthians had called Paul a fool. So now he takes their term and turns *fool* into a virtue and then boasts about his foolishness (11:1, 16, 17, 19, 21; 12:6, 11)! How do you counter someone who turns praise terms into derogatory terms, and derogatory terms into praise terms? Your gaping jaw might not close quickly enough to utter a response.

To grasp what Paul is doing, we need to have the ears of the Corinthians so we can accurately hear what he was saying to them. Not only did the term *fool* scratch the chalkboard in the Jewish world, where it was the opposite of wisdom (think Proverbs), but also the Corinthians would have heard that term with Greek and Roman ears, and such a claim did nothing but utterly degrade a speaker's status. A speaker truly claiming to be the fool would be ignored and ridiculed, which is exactly what Paul is doing to himself to confront the Corinthians with their Roman values. I am reminded of Leo Tolstoy's famous, short, parable-like story "The Story of Iván the Fool," who embodied antimilitarism and antigreed anticapitalism in a way of life that embraced the peasants, community, hospitality, and non-retaliation.[3] Tolstoy's story protests against the ways of the upper class Russians and the systemic injustices endured by peasants and serfs. In his essay, Tolstoy chooses a fool to be the hero who dismantles the wisdom of Russia's world.

Perhaps some of the Corinthians were surprised that Paul fought back against his seemingly Jewish Christian rivals with these "weak" arguments. Paul claims his pedigree matches up with anything his rivals have to offer: He is a Hebrew and an Israelite and a descendant of Abraham (11:22). He claims his calling in Christ (11:23). To complete his arguments, Paul connects his ministry not to some triumphal parade through a city but to the crucifixion theme. In all this he is butting heads with the status concerns of his critics, whose ideals of status come from Rome and Athens, not Jerusalem. His words deserve to be quoted and read, with a reminder that he is defending himself to Corinthians who are "wannabe Romans with status," as he addresses his Jewish Christian rivals' criticisms. In the following, I have reformatted Paul's words to better indicate the structure of his mind and logic:

> Since many boast consistent with flesh, I also will boast.
>
> For you, being prudent ones, put up with pleasure the "imprudent ones."
>
> For you put up if someone enslaves you,
> if someone gobbles [you] up,
> if someone takes [you],

if someone elevates [one's status],

if someone beats your face.

I say this consistent with dishonor, because we have been "weakened." In which [confident boasting], if someone dares—I speak in imprudence—I also dare:

Are they "Hebraioi [Hebrews]"? I am also.

Are they "Yisraēlitai [Israelites]"? I am also.

Are they "Abra'am's seed"? I am also.

Are they "Christos's servants"? (I speak contrary to prudence.)

I am more:

abundingly in labors,
aboundingly in prisons,
excessively in plagues,
often in deaths.
By Youdaians [Judeans, Jews], five times I received
    forty-minus-one [lashes].
Three times I was flogged.
Once I was stoned.
Three times I was shipwrecked.
For a night and a day I was rolling in the deep [sea].
Often on journeys,
    in dangers of rivers,
    in dangers of bandits,
    in dangers from [my own] ethnic group,
    in dangers from ethnic groups,
    in dangers in a city,
    in dangers in a desert,
    in dangers in a sea,
    in dangers with false siblings,
    in labor and fatigue,

often in sleeplessness, in hunger and thirst,
often in fastings, in cold and nakedness.

Apart from the exceptions [to the above] [there is] my daily supervision, [that is], the anxiety for all the assemblies.

Who weakens and I don't weaken?

Who trips and I am not set on fire?

If it's necessary to boast, I will boast about my weaknesses.

(The God and Father of the Lord Yēsous has known—who is blessed into the Eras—that I am not falsifying.)

In Damaskos [Damascus], Aretas the king's ethnarch was guarding the city of Damaskos to catch me, and through a window, in a basket, I was lowered through the wall, and I fled from his hands. (11:18–33)

I've italicized what I believe to be the most important line in the whole list, which reads, "If it's necessary to boast, I will boast about my weaknesses." Paul turns boasting's usual suspects—military, physical, economic, and oratorical status markers—on their heads. He fights back by flopping (or fawning) before their categories, only to arise with a Christoform set of counterintuitive credentials. The very events that intensified Paul's trauma become his school of spiritual transformation. When they accuse Paul of not acting the part, he looks them in the eye, with his feet planted from toes to heels, and says, "No, you are not acting the part."

But Paul's not done. Now that he has unrolled this foolish-boasting script, he brags about someone else (a veiled reference to himself). This man "was snatched up to third heaven" (12:2) to hear "unutterable utterances that are not permissible for a human to speak" (12:4). He's willing to boast about such a person, but he will not boast for himself. Everyone recognizes this person is Paul, a Paul who was out of the body, who is not the Paul they know. And we learn a secret about Paul as well. To discipline Paul from boasting about his spiritual experience, he divulges what he can, remaining metaphorical enough that we still debate what he is really talking about (12:7–9). Notice how Paul explains it: What God permits in his life is designed to keep him from exalting himself in status by revealing all he has seen in the heavens: "Therefore, so I may not raise my status."

To keep him in line, to constrain him, God gave him "a thorn-piercing-the-flesh." His clarification confuses us more today than it would have in his world, where spirits, *daimonia*, and angels populated the space between God and humans, and were at times evil and at other times good. His clarification is that this is "a Satanas [Satan]-envoy." Paul is almost certainly suggesting that God sent this "Satan-envoy" to him "to punch" him. Why? Again, "so I would not raise my status." God's promise is that his "grace" will be "enough," which leads Paul back to his short chorus: "I will boast with pleasure in my weaknesses." (All of this is from 12:7–9.)

Through such a thorn, Paul has learned to "take delight in weaknesses, in assaults, in necessities, in chases and distresses, for Christos" (12:10). He has learned through these experiences that when he is "weakened," he is most "empowered" (12:10). They have forced him to flip boasting into foolishness and to list all of his sufferings. He then adds even more: fighting back, complicating his strategy not to boast, by (yes) boasting about the presence of "authenticating signs," miracles, in his ministry (12:11–12).

Responding to Criticisms About Favoritism

Everybody has their favorites. Sometimes churches with several regular preachers don't announce in advance who will be preaching because, well, because people have their favorites. When their favorite is not slated to preach, they stay home. Leaders in churches have favorites too.

Teachers have their favorite students in a class, and students have their favorite teachers. Enrollment figures establish the truth of favorites. But favoritism is not the same as simply having favorites. Favoritism is when someone favors another person or persons so much that injustices, neglect, or prejudices appear. Favoritism is bias in favor of a particular person or group.

The various named leaders in Corinth could appear to be competing with one another—for the largest audience or the biggest givers or the most celebrated members meeting in the finest villas with the most slaves and the best food and the most expensive wines. Today's pastors live with this kind of competition in ways never seen before. You and I can open a laptop, wander into YouTube, and view the sermons of the most gifted preachers of our day. Easily. Daily. All day long. And most pastors don't measure up to that.

There's the pastor faithfully serving in a city with a wonderful congregation of about two hundred, but he knows people sometimes jet from his church to that church in the suburbs that draws two thousand. This pastor sometimes feels like he needs to compete with the pastor of that larger church, but a good pastor doesn't want to charm his congregants for their support. Nor should he. But still, they feel like they have to at times. Because people make comments, people insinuate problems, people suggest areas of improvement. Plus, those YouTube pastors' sermons are better and their musicians more gifted. The competition is all about the appeal of personality and appearance.

Favoritism works both ways too. People may favor a particular leader, while leaders may favor specific people. Think, again, of a pastor. Many pastors probably served a different church prior to accepting the call at their current church. And at times they will inevitably compare the churches. Sometimes they give the previous church a more favorable rating, and those in the current church may resent such comparisons and respond by expressing a preference for the previous pastor. The comparison game can go downhill quickly.

In Paul's Corinth, some people favored other leaders, say Apollos or Peter, and Paul countered with positive words—about his other mission churches. We know that at least some of the Corinthians were drawn to personalities performing on the platform who pleased their rhetorical palettes. If the Corinthian house churches could attract public speakers, they likely would increase their rank among the higher-status folks of this wannabe-like-Rome city. Groups, whether civic or academic or business, that could "hire" a philosopher or teacher were ranked above those that could not. Paul had refused to be their resident theologian, and Corinth felt shame when he refused to accept funds from them. Their shame intensified when it became clear in Corinth that Paul was accepting funds from Macedonia. "What are we, chopped liver?" the Corinthians muttered. Paul's response to the Corinthians provides glimpses of their allegations (11:5–11). Their allegation was Paul's favoritism: They believed he favored churches other than Corinth.

The Corinthians, for their part, were evidently drawn to teachers or apostles Paul pejoratively labeled as "superlative." Through leaks in Corinth, Paul was hearing them claim that they were on the same level of gifting, skill, and pastoral authority as Paul. These so-called superlatives accused Paul of being "self-taught," and by not accepting funds and instead doing manual labor to provide for himself and his coworkers, they felt Paul had degraded his status—and theirs by association. We know Paul decided to do manual labor intentionally, if not provocatively. But by degrading his status, he degraded theirs. Even worse, his critics invented an allegation against his management of money: The Corinthians said that in not accepting their funds and accepting the generous funds from the Macedonians, Paul "plundered" those from whom he received donations. They accused him of not loving them.

They were convinced Paul played favorites, and those favorite churches and people clearly resided elsewhere than Corinth.

How does Paul respond? Again, Paul fights for himself. His response is clinical in its logic. If the Corinthians reject him and prefer the superlative apostles, Paul, willing and able now to compare himself to the superlatives, tells them "[that I] 'lack' nothing" (11:5). They say he's self-taught. In response he briefly grants their point but one-ups them by claiming he's got their prized possession on his side: "knowledge" (*gnosis*; 11:6). He jabs them with a stiff reminder when he says his knowledge was abundantly clear when he taught them in their presence. Money and status are never out of their minds, so he reminds them that he chose to preach to them "as a gift" (11:7). To be sure, Paul's decision to be a manual laborer in Corinth is a status-lowering action.[4] And because Paul does not take funds from a church until that church is stable and self-sufficient, his decision to receive funds from Macedonia, but not Corinth, has a not-so-hidden implication. Implicit in this back-and-forth is that by not taking money from the Corinthians, Paul is implying that they are not stable and self-sufficient. Put more bluntly, they are *un*stable and *in*sufficient. Paul counters that he is not playing favorites but that he operates under his own conditions of ministry, playing by the rules he and his associates have formed over time spent planting churches. Paul feels he has explained himself to his own satisfaction.

In their book *Wounded Pastors*, Carol Howard and James Fenimore tell the story of a pastor they name "Betsy." When Betsy opens her email one day, she discovers the intended unintentional email called "Minutes from Board Meeting." I describe it as "intended unintentional" because this email was sent as a passive-aggressive act by someone on the board she worked alongside in leading the church. Betsy was supposed to moderate all board meetings, but she was not invited to this particular meeting. The reason she was not invited was because the board had voted six for and five against a motion to fire her, with one abstention. "Through the sterile language of the minutes, she reads how the board secretary received a letter from a wealthy family threatening to leave the congregation if the board did not fire Betsy immediately. She sits back in her chair and tries to recall how she offended the family."

It is a done deal, of course. But Betsy digs in her heels and insists that she continue pastoring there until she can find another church. Those are difficult months for her, with the deepest challenge being forgiveness. "She isn't sure how she is going to let this one go. How can she forgive the board members when they never showed any remorse? How can she let go of her resentment when they never apologized? And what about her sense of justice? Don't they deserve some sort of punishment for treating her so terribly? It didn't seem like they were going to get any sort of retribution, so at the very least, they should have to deal with her resentment."[5]

Betsy is not the only pastor or church leader who has experienced a surprise release. Firing someone is at best awkward and at worst a gut-wrenching process. Yet Christians are called to do the right thing, and the right thing is to prepare the person for that day by going through an honest, transparent process of evaluation, giving them steps for development, an assessment or evaluation, followed by more steps and more evaluation, all attended to with professional tact and pastoral care. And, I would add, buttressed by a trauma-informed approach to termination. Sudden firings are not the way of Christ. And forgiveness becomes far more difficult when the process is not transparent. If a person doing the firing has little experience in doing so, there will often be some missteps. In those situations, they should apologize rather than defend themselves.

My guess here (I hope) is accurate: The Corinthians did not go through a reasonable process of evaluating Paul. Like Betsy, Paul was traumatized by their treatment of him, but he stood his ground and fought back.

Responding to Criticisms About No Longer Being Special

Christian leaders who step down, step aside, or step out of the picture quickly experience a loss of status. It's inevitable. A professor friend of mine, when I was discussing with him that I was considering teaching at a different institution, observed to me with a flick of a finger, "In two years the student body will not even remember you." He added, "Ask me, I know the experience." Oy, that was a cold splash of reality in my face.

Losing status is predictable. That doesn't make it easy. Status is precious to leaders. Sometimes too precious. Paul knew the Corinthians had their own favorites—some liked Apollos or Peter more than him. Some laid claim to be what looks like the first variant of a "Jesus only" group. Sometimes those who lay claims like that are more anti-someone than pro-Jesus, but that's another story. A crucial expression almost certainly quotes a slogan Paul's critics used: "just like us" (11:12). As the NIV translates, "And I will keep on doing what I am doing in order to cut the ground from under those who want an opportunity to be considered equal with us in the things they boast about." The NIV's "equal with us" expresses our "just like us" translation. The ones criticizing Paul claimed they were the authorities (or apostles) of Corinth too.

Perhaps so, but that's not the major problem. Christian churches can flourish with multiple leaders. The problem for Paul was not multiple leaders. What unnerved him was that his own children in the faith had disowned him and attached themselves to other leaders. We can guess that at least some who switched their allegiance had lined up as Peter-ites or Apollos-ites. But let's be blunt: Tenderhearted Paul experienced rejection in their choice to be led by others.

Paul's response? Anger, expressed in fighting back yet again (11:12–15). Traumatized persons fight back out of anger and resentment, and a healthy anger serves to remind us that we have suffered an injustice. Paul's fight in these verses is not pretty to watch: He indicates his desire to "chop off" the "opportunity" his critics have in wanting to level themselves with him. He calls them names: "false Commissioners, deceitful workers, reshaping themselves into Christos's Commissioners." These are clear slurs against his critics, slurs designed to identify true leaders (himself and his associates) and to lead the Corinthians away from false leaders. Paul jams the shovel even deeper into the muck when he connects these "false leaders" to "Satanas," who "reshapes [himself] into a light-envoy." How do these alternative authorities understand themselves? Paul describes their attempts to "reshape themselves as rightness-servants." The labels Paul uses are the ultimate degradation; he has assigned them to evil.[6] How do we explain such brutal language? Trauma.

Trauma yearns to express itself, just as those who have experienced injustice ache for justice. Not all expressions of this longing for justice are tender, nice, and pretty. At times it can get ugly. Paul got ugly when he began calling his opponents names, and ugly often attends trauma. My (Scot) contention is that if we listen with empathy to Paul's ugliness in these chapter, we will gain further insight into Paul's condition. As we've noted, he's in the trauma zone, but this does not excuse Paul or legitimate ugly slurs of others. What it does is help us better understand the responses of those who have been traumatized and why they act and speak as they do when they've been hurt.

Chapter 8

Listening to Emotions

Anger, Safety, Self-Defense, Affirming Trauma

Sarcasm expresses anger. At times it can be bitter, at times sardonic, and at times almost jocular when one dismisses something in an almost helpless manner. If we dig underneath the sarcasm, however, we typically find anger. Christians are sometimes taught that anger is wrong, that they need to control their emotions, and that losing control means a person has some significant spiritual work to do. Christians who teach that anger is wrong are wrong, because the Bible's major figures are at times angry.

Yes, even Jesus was angry: "He looked around at them in anger and, deeply distressed at their stubborn hearts, said to the man . . ." (Mark 3:5 NIV). The disciples were angry, though the NIV uses a more dignified term for it when it translates "some of those present were saying indignantly to one another, 'Why this waste of perfume?'" (Mark 14:4 NIV). Paul legitimated anger, at least for a time, when he wrote these words to the Ephesians: "In your anger do not sin: Do not let the sun go down while you are still angry" (Eph. 4:26 NIV). Notice what that opening line assumes: There is such a thing as sinless anger. Paul warns, too, about the rages of anger (4:31; Col. 3:8), and the brother of Jesus says that "human anger does not produce the righteousness that God desires" (James 1:20 NIV). The upshot is this: There's a right time to be angry, and a wrong time to be angry. More to the point, legitimate anger needs to be contained and constrained.

Anger is an emotion, and God designed and created us to have emotions. Emotions are good. Emotionlessness is not good. Anger expresses our emotions of irritation and frustration, and it comes out because of sadness or shame or guilt or fear. Even more anger comes to the surface over injustices done to us. As the Vancouver Island University website says, referring to workplace conflict, "Anger is a feeling that is normal and healthy, and serves the function of letting us know when all is not right in our world."[1] The site helpfully includes a map of the "anger arousal cycle" as well:

> The arousal cycle of anger has five phases: trigger, escalation, crisis, recovery and depression. Understanding the cycle helps us to understand our own reactions and those of others.
>
> - *The trigger phase* is when an event gets the anger cycle started. We get into an argument or receive some information that shocks us. We feel threatened at some level and our physiological system prepares to meet that threat.
> - *The escalation phase* is when our body prepares for a crisis with increased respiration (rapid breathing), increased heart rate and raised blood pressure, muscles tense for action, voice may become louder or an altered pitch, and our eyes change shape, pupils enlarge and brow falls. Take note of these things next time you feel angry. Your body stance may change as well.
> - *The crisis phase* is when our survival instinct steps in, the fight or

flight response. Our body is prepared to take action. Unfortunately, during this phase our quality of judgment is significantly reduced and decisions may be made without the benefit of the best reasoning ability.

- *The recovery phase* takes place after some action has resulted during the crisis phase. The body starts to recover from the extreme stress and expenditure of energy. The adrenaline in our blood leaves gradually. Quality of judgment returns as reasoning begins to replace the survival response.
- *The post-crisis depression phase* is the point when the body enters a short period in which the heart rate slips below normal so the body can regain its balance. Awareness and energy return to allow us to assess what just happened. We may begin to feel guilt, regret, or emotional depression.

Here we find an intelligent plotting of what many traumatized persons experience. The longer a person suppresses her anger, the greater the likelihood that she will enter the trauma zone of depression. She needs increasing levels of energy to hold back anger until she reaches the point when there's no energy left. We call this phase "depression." And as surprising as it may sound, expressing anger can actually start the healthy journey toward healing.

Christians ought to be angry about injustice. We should be angry over the sexual enslavement of young girls, the unleashing of gun violence in schools, reckless abuse against women in homes and in public, pastors preying on those in their care, fathers who neglect or abuse their children, parents who bring children into homes filled with drug addictions, and politicians who lie and manipulate and cannot seem to answer a question with transparent truth telling. Yes, anger has its place. Those who have been abused and wounded, especially those who have stored up their wounds in silence and suppression, should not be told it is wrong to feel angry. Christians wound other Christians, and many wounded Christians will go through a phase of feeling anger at the person who has traumatized them and over the actions of their abusers. There's a right time to be angry. When we are wronged, it's right to feel anger. Paul got angry when he was in the trauma zone because he was being treated unjustly. He perceived he was unsafe and felt a need for safety.

Anger as a Strategy to Find Some Safety

Many readers of Paul's hot takes in 2 Corinthians fail to recognize he is using a form of irony called sarcasm.[2] Matthew Pawlak, who is an expert on detecting sarcasm and irony in ancient texts, has a maxim that requires our respect: "Simply put, taking a sarcastic utterance literally or reading a literal utterance sarcastically both have the potential to generate serious misreadings of a text."[3] I (Scot) believe many have misread Paul here. Their misreadings, instead of revealing Paul's wounded heart, become a license for them to abuse others with similar language. Irony and sarcasm do not describe a situation accurately. When they are wrongly assumed to be accurate and are used to abuse others, they are doubly inaccurate. Because we read these chapters in 2 Corinthians without noticing Paul's sarcasm, I want to slow us down to draw out some of the instances of Paul's use of sarcasm and more closely examine them.

Sarcasm is "a subset of verbal irony in which an utterance that would normally communicate a positive attitude or evaluation implies a negative attitude or evaluation."[4] We see self-deprecating irony in texts like 2 Corinthians 10:1, where Paul says "I . . . who am 'timid' when face to face with you, but 'bold' toward you when away!" (NIV). These words are not an accurate description of Paul's behaviors but rather his use of the Corinthians' words to slur him. There's no chance Paul thinks of himself as timid or a wallflower. And while these words self-deprecate, because they are sarcastic in tone they communicate he doesn't believe they express one syllable of truth. Nor does Paul think he has made a fool of himself (12:11), nor does he think he needs forgiveness when he says, "Forgive me this wrong!" (12:13 NIV). That's how sarcasm works. And remember, sarcasm is one way we express our anger.

Unless words are clearly expressed in a tone of anger, it takes skill to recognize sarcasm. One time on a speaking trip, my wife, Kris, and I (Scot) went to lunch with a young man who had published a couple of books. It was a pleasant enough lunch and we had an enjoyable chat with him. On our way home, Kris, who is a psychologist, said, "Wow, is he an angry man." I was a bit surprised, so I asked why she said that. Kris answered, "So many of his statements were framed in sarcasm. Sarcasm," she said to me, "often expresses anger." As we reflected over our luncheon, I recalled a number of his sarcastic comments. I had not noticed such comments while reading his books, but then again, editors often remove most sarcasm because it can be hard to spot and easy to misread. Kris had spotted it and I had misread it!

Paul utilizes sarcastic self-promotion in 2 Corinthians. Frustration and irritation lead to anger, and anger is typical of trauma. Many who are traumatized speak with sarcasm. Some more than others, some too often, others perhaps not often enough. A therapist will frequently tell the traumatized that it's okay to be angry. If you are angry, you are angry. Suppressing anger isn't healthy, though some ways of expressing anger are not as healthy as others. I'm not sure Paul always expressed his trauma in the best way. But express it he did.

To give you a better experience of Paul's sarcasm, read 2 Corinthians 11:16–21 in a sarcastic tone. Make it a hot mic moment. (If you can't find your sarcastic voice, find a deconstructer in your church and he or she will show you how to read it. Deconstructors know sarcasm.) In the following quotation, I have put the words to be spoken with sarcasm in scare quotes. Notice how Paul fades out of sarcasm at the end into self-deprecating irony.

> I say again, let no one think of me as "an imprudent one." But if you think otherwise, receive me as an "imprudent one" so I may also "boast" a little bit. What I am speaking, I am not speaking—in "this boasting's substance"—consistent with Lord but as "in imprudence." Since many "boast" consistent with flesh, I also will "boast."
>
> For you, being "prudent ones," put up with pleasure the "imprudent ones."
>
> For you put up
>
> if someone "enslaves" you,
> if someone "gobbles [you] up,"
> if someone "takes [you],"
> if someone "elevates [status],"
> if someone "beats your face."
>
> I say this consistent with "dishonor," because we have been "weakened." In which [confident boasting], if someone dares—I speak in "imprudence—I also dare . . .

Most of us are skilled enough to detect moments of sarcasm, but no one can miss the heavy sarcasm of these verses when they are read with the right tone. Pawlak sums up why Paul turns to his self-promotion in 2 Corinthians: "I suggest that one may explain this correlation quite simply by taking it as a sign of Paul's frustration. He sees himself as being forced to promote himself in ways that he is not comfortable with, which irritates him, prompting a sarcastic response when the subject of his boasting arises."[5]

Pawlak intensifies Paul's emotions by describing the situation brilliantly. Paul's status was being challenged; he fought back to preserve his status and honor, in the hope that the Corinthians would revise their estimation of him and, in so doing, he would return to a safe relationship with them. Pawlak begins with the situation:

> The situation is well established: Paul's opponents have challenged his authority and his congregation is in danger of shifting their allegiance.

Then Pawlak turns to Paul's sarcasm:

> Paul's use of sarcasm shows that he does not accept the threatened loss of face, as he responds by presuming the authority that his opponents seek to deny him.

Then he explains why Paul turns up the sarcasm knob:

> The fact that Paul's sarcasm targets both his congregation and his opponents, then, suggests two things. First, it implies that he seeks to retain the superior, apostolic position from which it is appropriate for him to make sarcastic comments to his churches. Second, Paul's sarcasm aims to challenge his congregation's and rivals' attempts to situate themselves higher than they ought to vis-à-vis himself.

In Paul's and the Corinthians' context—and both Paul and the Corinthians understood how rhetoric works—sarcasm expresses vehement anger:

> These aims are well described in Hermogenes, who associates sarcasm with *a vehement style* that makes use of strong criticism to reproach one's subordinates.[6]

Pawlak's mentioning of Hermogenes, whom he discusses elsewhere in his study, scores the point: Sarcasm and anger are tied together. Which leads us also to ask what emotions might be at work in Paul's self-deprecations. Again, Pawlak's summary enlightens us here (italics added for emphasis):

> In concert with the sarcastic side of Paul's rhetoric with its appropriation of authority and challenge to his opponents and congregation, Paul's use of *asteïsmos* [self-deprecating irony, *eirōneia*] adds another layer to his communication. This speech act is apologetic, implicitly rejecting perceived accusations while—if we accept Hermogenes' assessment—creating *a tone of offended indignation*. Such *barytēs* [indignation] should weigh heavily on any conscience that still feels allegiance or sympathy toward Paul, encouraging a recognition that Paul has been shamefully mistreated. While Paul's sarcasm presumes a position of authority, his more defensive use of *asteïsmos* shows his awareness of the threat to his position.[7]

Paul was in trouble in Corinth. He knew it. He was wounded by what he was hearing. It made him angry, and he went sarcastic in his response. We have dipped into sarcasm here at length (1) because Paul's sarcasm is often not even recognized by Bible readers and (2) because sarcasm expresses indignation and anger, and (3) that means Paul's response to the trauma zone included anger. Anger is a healthy emotion in response to trauma.

Defending Yourself as a Strategy to Find Safety

Paul presents himself as one who refuses to defend himself. He asks the Corinthians, and he doesn't think he needs an answer, this question:

"Have you been thinking all along that we have been defending ourselves to you?" (12:19 NIV; cf. 3:1; 5:12). This is why Paul earlier denied his own acts of self-promotion. He asked, "Are we beginning to commend ourselves?" and another time he denied it, saying, "We are not trying to commend ourselves" (3:1; 5:12 NIV). Paul can say what he wants here, but most ordinary readers see this as self-defense, if not self-promotion. People who put pen to papyrus to write the following words have to admit there's at least some defensiveness in what they communicate:

> Now this is our boast: Our conscience testifies that we have conducted ourselves in the world, and especially in our relations with you, with integrity and godly sincerity. (1:12 NIV)

> Rather, we have renounced secret and shameful ways; we do not use deception, nor do we distort the word of God. On the contrary, by setting forth the truth plainly we commend ourselves to everyone's conscience in the sight of God. (4:2 NIV)

> Rather, as servants of God we commend ourselves in every way. (6:4 NIV)

You can't write these things and deny you are being defensive. One is hard pressed to read the last four chapters of this letter, especially with their display of Paul's self-styled foolish boasting, as anything other than Paul's defense of himself. The tension between the denial and the reality is noticeable. N. T. Wright's own summary comparison of 1 and 2 Corinthians is about as good as one can get: "the second letter to Corinth is not only . . . quite different in style (at least for several chapters) from Paul's other letters. It is also jerkier and its overall structure, with what appear to be false starts, extra paragraphs injected into the argument, sudden resumptions of earlier themes, and not least a sudden change of mood toward the end, as it goes from the agonized and halting early chapters to a sudden combative, teasing, and upbeat conclusion."[8] No doubt, some of the congregation's critics of Paul in Corinth considered his peculiar letter's arguments as solid as a soufflé. In 2 Corinthians 10–13 Paul alternates between fighting back with words and fawning before the Corinthians in an attempt to make himself more appealing.

Affirming Your Trauma to Find Safety

It may help us to have trauma therapists reading over our shoulders and whispering in our ears if we want to hear accurately what Paul says to the Corinthians. Adrienne and I (Scot) believe not only that trauma theory helps us to better understand Paul but also that Paul's responses can be passages of empathy for those who have been traumatized by fellow Christians. Anger and defensiveness, two sides of the same coin, are indicators that permit us to recognize trauma in someone. With these two style choices briefly described, we will now use insights from trauma theory and attempt to sketch how Paul responds to the accusations against him. How Paul responds corresponds to how many of us today would like to respond when we have been traumatized by Christians with unjust, public accusations. However, if most of us responded to criticism as Paul does in these four chapters, we would be dismissed, suppressed, ignored, or even released, sacked, or fired. Many of our churches today would not tolerate Paul's displays of anger. Christians, especially leaders at every level in any Christian organization, are expected to take it, absorb it, deflect it, and live above it. The "it" can be verbal or emotional abuse. "Criticism comes with the turf," we hear.

But burying one's feelings is the surest way to enter depression and anxiety. God designed us to dwell in safety, and our God-given instincts lead us to want a safe place when we are in trauma. Entering the trauma zone means realizing that we have experienced something and are dealing with some lasting reminders of the experience. We need to recognize trauma, and this means we need to be in tune with our bodies and how they feel. We need to be aware when something leads us to feel off or we are responding to situations in ways that confuse us or leave us frustrated at our words or actions. If something is poking at us about how we are behaving, we need to take a deeper look. We need to be aware and reflective, recognizing that something momentous or difficult has happened to us by affirming our experiences and honoring them. This is how we move toward healing and health.

When my (Adrienne) family moved home from an almost three-year stint in Portland, I knew we all had experienced trauma. Instead of seeing it while it was happening, I spent that time trauma-comparing, telling myself that what we were experiencing was not as bad as what some of our friends were going through. We did not lose our house like some of our friends did. We did not lose a child like some of our friends did. So I put off doing my own trauma work. When I finally went to see my therapist six months after moving home, I thought things were much better. I shared with this professional what we had lived through, and she looked at me and said, "You have experienced a great deal of trauma in a short time." My body needed to hear those words. They let me affirm my trauma, giving me permission to finally acknowledge our experience. It was important for me to both recognize and affirm that I had experienced trauma. And it was helpful to hear those words from another person, especially a trained professional.

Many people in our churches, families, and communities have experienced trauma. Much of it goes unrecognized and unacknowledged, as mine did for many months. As we think about how to help people in these circumstances, we want to turn in the next section to look closely at what is needed to nurture trauma-safe spaces. How do we cultivate space for people to recognize that they have been traumatized and then to heal from that trauma?

PART 3

Trauma Safe

THE EYES

Chapter 9

Safety

Church folks inflict wounds on other church folks, including leaders. To be sure, many leaders bear the brunt of their congregations' criticisms, but trauma is no respecter of persons. It deposits itself in the hearts and souls of many. Trauma has been systemic in church cultures, and it will be until church folks put a stop to it, or at least slow it down. We believe there is an opportunity to nurture cultures that are trauma informed, trauma sensitive, trauma safe, and trauma free. Taking advantage of this opportunity will require both realizing what trauma is and recognizing the symptoms of trauma.

A friend of mine (Scot) is a pastor who was living in a church culture that promoted abuse (of this pastor friend of mine) and demanded blanket agreement, or the parishioners would take their tithes and offerings and walk out. The church he served is far from unique, and his story could be repeated with slight variations by many church leaders. We share his words not only to express his trauma but also—and there is good news here—to prompt us to think about how we can nurture safer cultures.

> If a system had been designed specifically to abuse pastors, it couldn't do the job any better than what we know today as the modern pastorate. For one, it is almost entirely one-sided in the mind of churchgoers. Pastors are expected to show up at our darkest moments and offer theological insight, wisdom, and empathy (this is both good and important), while a breakup email is all that is necessary to let the pastor know they have moved on. No reason is necessary and often none is given. Less than ten people during my tenure here have left our church after having a face-to-face conversation with me. Most just seem to be raptured away.

God designed our bodies to protect themselves. Anger can be a tunnel into safety and protection. So we want to say this: It's okay to be angry, because at times ugly gonna do ugly and anger gonna do anger. We are not advocating an ugly anger that explodes into vindictiveness, fumigating the sanctuary with rage, and neither do we advocate revenge. But self-protection is a virtue, and every human deserves safety.

My (Scot) study of the apostle Paul continues to surprise me. Five years ago, I never would have used the terms *PTSD* and *trauma* in connection with Paul. Yet reading Adrienne's master's thesis led me, during my writing of the Everyday Bible Study on 2 Corinthians, to see Paul with fresh eyes. Because of Adrienne's thesis I began to see things in Paul I had not noticed before, things that were present in the text but that I had not recognized. I had glimpsed them, but I explained them without nuance, as in "Paul's emotions get the best of him here." Adrienne's thesis gave me the tools to see what I had only glimpsed. I now see what I had not seen. As we turn in this section to look at how Paul responded to his trauma and how the gospel reshaped Paul's response to trauma, we want to begin by exploring the divine design for safety.

Relational Safety

Safety is the number one virtue, practice, and habit for a trauma-informed community. It is the first pillar in a trauma-sensitive environment because safety is required if you want to nurture a trauma-free zone. If an individual coming into your community or working within your community does not feel safe, no other ideas, practices, and habits will matter. Safety is essential because humans heal in the context of relationship and community. And we need safety within that community to properly heal and to help other people heal. The necessity of safety for healing in community should spur us to form safe environments and relationships.

Let's come back to a statement we dropped in the previous paragraph: We heal in the context of relationship and community. When we are harmed in a community, it is challenging to heal in the context of (sometimes the same) community. Safety has been shattered by the abuse we have suffered. A person does not have to announce "I have been wounded" or "I am in the trauma zone" for trauma to be present. Most of us hide our trauma and are silent about it.

Many feel shame. Shame is "the intensely painful feeling or experience of believing we are flawed and therefore unworthy of acceptance and belonging."[1] Shame emotes from our experiences, and these experiences lead us to seek safety to survive. Survival, safety, and shame can form a network in our inner worlds, unknown to us, perhaps, but still present. When we find ourselves in unsafe or abusive situations, our survival and seek-safety instincts may kick in, but a sense of shame often lingers within us, even once we find some measure of safety. We may feel shame for thinking someone is safe and trusting them, only to learn that person is harmful or toxic. As Tricia Lott Williford and Jana Richardson have written, "many victims feel an agonizing shame from the actions they took to survive, and then even more shame because of the connection they maintained with the person who abused them. Especially if the abuser was close to the victim, someone they relied on, the victim might feel confused about whether they were a victim or a willing participant. This muddies the margin between feelings and fear, between pain and pleasure."[2] A traumatized individual often has to work through the shame they feel because of some of the things they may have done in the midst of trauma. Maybe your director or pastor or leader was demanding, abusive, and harsh with a coworker, and now you perceive yourself as complicit in some of that abusive behavior. You may feel shame over what "we" have done, even if you know deep in your heart that the abuse was precipitated by the leader. Maybe you are afraid to own not only your complicity but your co-abusive behaviors. The emotion experienced here is often shame, and it is often unknown to others.

Imagine a small group that has been meeting for many months and has started to form a small community. Some will feel safe in that community and may have felt safe from the very beginning. These people often have little to no trauma in their background. Their nervous systems have not had to go into survival mode very often. They came into this group wanting to form a bond and study the Bible with others. They are open and willing to trust others.

Now let's add to this group a few dominating voices who like to take charge and oversee the group. Their postures do not bother the individuals who can easily form safe and secure attachments. Even if members who feel safe get cut off or overlooked, they brush it off and let it go. They have had many prior positive experiences in small groups, and they are expecting this one to be the same.

But let's consider adding some to this group who may not feel safe. They enter both the group and the conversations in the group with caution. They likely have heightened nervous systems and have had to fight to survive abuse in relationships a few times. They do not trust easily. Those few dominating voices are enough for them to remain in the background and patiently watch. Perhaps these dominant individuals remind them of strict or harsh behaviors they faced in the past. This group does not feel safe to them. The size doesn't matter; it may be large or it may be small. Each person instinctively knows whether the group is safe, and this sense of safety often determines how they will participate.

How do we help a person who struggles with feeling safe move toward safety? First, safety needs to be defined by the person seeking it. If someone wants to know what helps me (Adrienne) feel safe, they need to ask. If I want to know how to help Scot feel safe, I have to ask. Safety is defined by those who do not hold the power.[3] The simple task of asking others to inform us is key, showing up again and again when you study trauma-informed principles. We ask what safety means to someone and then listen and act accordingly. This nurtures a culture of safety. When you let the hurting person determine what is safe for themselves, you give them their voice back. You give them a distinct humanness. They are not you, and you should not assume that you are the same. You also give them a sense of agency. Agency and autonomy permit someone to define safety for themselves. Regaining their voice in this instance may be one slow and small way you can rebuild a sense of safety. Though it may seem small, it may have the largest impact on that person.

Keep in mind that safety is both physical and emotional. The first is more obvious. The second is more complicated and requires further explanation. Let's take a look at each.

Physical Safety

Physical safety is what most companies, ministries, and organizations think of when the word *safety* is used. A person needs to feel physically safe, and when a body goes into fight, flight, freeze, or fawn mode, that body no longer feels safe. Hypervigilance sets in and the person constantly scans the environment looking for an escape to safety, looking for the next possible threat. Persons in the trauma zone are on high alert.

No church or ministry wants a person to be on constant alert or feel under threat when they walk through their doors. There are many little things that churches and organizations can do to make someone feel calm and safe.

First, the campus or the building needs to embody physical safety. It is easy for an able-bodied person to forget or overlook what physical safety looks and feels like for a person who cannot simply walk into a building. Is your church or ministry handicapped equipped? The quickest way to find out is to ask the people who can answer this question. Check in with those who have different needs and abilities, including those who are elderly, in need of a walker or wheelchair, or stricken with arthritis. Ask them to come to your campus or building and be ready to hear their feedback about what their experience was like, even if it is critical. Listen and don't become defensive; rather, seek to learn.

Physical safety also includes the way buildings and offices are designed and marked. Fire and emergency exits should be visible, legible, and accessible to all. Someone who has been held hostage or felt stuck in a domestic-violence situation will need to feel they can leave or escape immediately. When someone on staff meets with a visitor or congregant, do you meet in large open spaces, or in tight jammed offices? Who sits closest to the door? You may have never thought about these matters, but abused persons do, even if subconsciously. I (Adrienne) once received a call from a clinician who was in an office right below me. When I picked up the phone, she told me she needed help and asked if I would come to her office. Slightly confused, I walked down the hall and then down the stairs to her office. When I arrived, I knocked on the door and opened it and saw that a large teenage male was standing between her and the door. He was clearly upset and told her she couldn't leave, blocking her from walking out the door. We were able to calm him down and open the door (which relieved the situation), but she changed her office layout after that day.

Office layouts matter. Look for a way to make sure everyone in the room feels physically safe. If I am not able to get up and open the door because of how I have positioned myself, I will not feel safe. Women often think about this more than men. If you are male and you have a female coming into your workspace, have you considered how safe they might feel in your environment? Are they closer to the door? Might they want the door open? If you knew it would help them feel safe, would you want them to sit closer to the door? Another option is to design the room so there are multiple places to sit. When someone enters your office, you can ask them where they would prefer to sit. Again, if you ask, you give them agency and you respect their ability to define it for themselves. Consider physical proximity as well, how close you sit to an individual. Ask them if they are comfortable with the space between you. I realize this may seem a long way from the conflict between Paul and the Corinthians, but it is not as far as it might seem. Paul would not have used our terms, but Paul was pursuing safety in his own way. The key takeaway is that an understanding of safety matters if we want to better understand trauma and how to form safe spaces for people.

Emotional Safety

People who attend your ministry, who volunteer, or who are paid to be there all need to feel safe physically, mentally, and emotionally. Emotional safety starts when a person listens to their God-designed body. We all need to learn what signals our bodies give us when we feel uncomfortable or threatened. We have to recognize that our bodies are trying to get our attention at times, but often we do not know how to listen. We may need to develop better emotional intelligence.

Much attention in the past has been focused on intelligence quotient, or IQ, but until recently there was not as much focus on a person's EQ, or emotional quotient. One aspect of emotional intelligence as it relates to our discussion of emotional safety is being able to, in the moment, realize you are feeling something and then discern what it is and whether there is anything you should do about it.

Discernment starts with knowing yourself and paying attention to your body. This is where most people struggle. Some people never really listen to their bodies, so take a moment right now to think about your body and what it tells you. Obviously, it tells you whether you are hungry, it tells you whether you are tired, and it tells you whether you have to use the restroom. We often assume these are things we think, but we actually feel them first. Our bodies talk to our brains and then tell us what to think. So if your body starts to feel hungry, that starts in your stomach and then the sensation communicates to your brain that you need to eat something. If you are tired, your body feels a sensation, maybe heaviness or lethargy, and your body sends a message to your brain that it is time to wind down. We can ignore these sensations, and we get good at doing that, but we know that over time we need to listen and pay attention and act or we will pay a price for ignoring our bodies.

Our bodies do the same thing with our emotions. They begin in our bodies. So if someone says something that hurts me, my body will feel that emotion, and then that feeling communicates to my brain that I am hurt or sad because of that comment. Unfortunately, we can learn to ignore these feelings, and then we fail to recognize them when we need to. Ignoring our emotions is a sign that we lack emotional intelligence and awareness, which often comes from not learning to listen to our bodies when we were younger. Many people grew up in families where they were not taught or it was not modeled how to listen to their bodies and let them guide them. Some were taught that emotions are unreliable guides, so they learned to stifle their feelings. Such persons need to work to learn what their bodies and feelings are communicating to them.

Let's say I am having a conversation with an individual. They are talking and talking, but suddenly I realize my brain is telling me to say something to get them to stop talking so I can leave. I cannot just think it through any further and stop listening and get out of there. But my emotional intelligence tells me to dig into what I am feeling and what this is all about. I listen to my body, asking myself, "What am I feeling?" I feel uncomfortable. I feel talked at. Okay, that's a good start, so let's dig deeper. I am feeling like they never let me talk. When I try to speak up, they interrupt me and keep talking. So I am feeling ignored and maybe even unimportant or overlooked. Now, that is a deeper, more intimate feeling. I have gone from knowing I feel uncomfortable in my body to realizing I am feeling overlooked and silenced. I also sense a feeling of avoidance. So instead of hightailing it out of there, I decide to say something. I tell them that they are interrupting me every time I try to say something and that I do not feel like I am actually needed in this conversation. They may stop talking and perhaps say, "That makes sense. I'll slow down." Or maybe not. Still, regardless of how they respond, I looked at my emotions, I paid attention to them, I discerned what I felt in my body, and I dug into what was going on inside me. I decided to take action and felt I could say something. I was heard and understood, and I also heard and understood myself.

You may still wonder, "What happens if they do not acknowledge your comment?" We cannot control how the person will respond, but please do not dismiss the hard work you did in yourself. You connected with your emotions and better understood yourself and your emotional response. When someone dismisses how you are feeling, they may be communicating that your emotions are not important to them. You now get to determine whether you feel safe in this relationship.

The good news is that you can work on this practice and develop it, and you can get really good at it. The bad news is that you are responsible to do it for yourself. No one can do it for you.

How does this relate to our conversation about safety and cultivating safe spaces? Safety is felt in the body. So when we feel unsafe in a room or with a person or with the tone that someone is using, our bodies are going to feel that lack of safety. It is important to know this about ourselves and to practice recognizing it, but it is also important to know that people may experience this lack of safety and not know what to do about it. If they need to leave or need to stop the conversation and they cannot fully communicate why, it may mean their bodies are communicating to them and they are trying to take action. They may need to feel safe again. We can try to give them what they need or what they want, and being trauma informed about emotional safety may mean we let them stop a conversation and leave.

Safety is and should be empowering. A survivor may be just getting her feet back under herself and taking first steps to reach out to be in community or conversation with others. Empowerment means helping them to learn to speak up and be heard. Each of us can learn to listen to ourselves and speak up. A person may be learning that he can be honest and not be abused. Or she is learning she can disagree with you and she will not be hit or yelled at or ignored. He can cry and no one will laugh at him or mock him. She can speak and someone is there to listen. He can rest and relax and not be punished for taking time for himself.

Being trauma informed is being aware of both our response and the response of others as they test out their need to feel safe. Can they disagree with something that has been done? Will we listen to them? Will it make us angry? When they see we are displeased, will we notice that they shrink away and hide or do whatever they can to make us happy again? How do we encourage thoughts and opinions? How easily do we assess what they may be doing and what they may need from us? Remember, when in doubt, ask. Remember, too, that we each need to determine what is safe for us.

Safety is the first pillar, built on a foundation of listening. Every single person in the relationship has to think through how safety applies to themselves personally. Do they feel it, inside their body and inside their place of work or ministry? That's the first step. Then we need to live out what we are learning and apply it to the people we come into contact with. Safety is a both/and. We work on it within ourselves, using it in our own lives, *and* we apply it outside ourselves as we relate to others. In fact, all of the trauma-informed pillars and principles apply to both the helper and the hurt. The helper, listener, and volunteer must feel safe within her life and within her place of work and with the people around her. As her sense of safety grows, she can work on helping other people feel and experience this sense of safety.

Safety is the first pillar. But let's not forget something we learn from Paul. Corinth was not a safe place for him, physically or emotionally, so he sought out safety in Ephesus with his coworkers and friends, with whom he felt safe. The next pillar looks at the importance of boundaries for forming safe spaces in churches. How do we establish boundaries that can help people heal from trauma?

Chapter 10

Boundaries

When we are in the trauma zone, we experience various kinds of loss, and these losses have ongoing effects and affects in our bodies. Clearly, we have a loss of safety. Fear and danger are now imprinted on our brains. "It is possible," Sandra Bloom writes, "that once fear is learned, it can never be 'unlearned' at a basic physiological level."[1] The world has changed into a place where anything can happen, and we know this because the unimaginable or unbelievable has occurred.

But we also have a loss of danger cues. When someone we trusted wounds us, we no longer trust ourselves with any level of confidence, and we may no longer be sure about who is safe and who is not safe. It becomes much easier to decide that everyone is unsafe. We have a loss of trust as well. If we've determined that everyone around us is now unsafe, it can be hard to decide how to trust people. We may determine we are no longer a good judge of character. We no longer trust ourselves and we no longer trust those around us. The longer this continues, the more difficult it is to figure out how to trust ourselves or others again. Often we do not fully comprehend how much safety and trust has been lost. So we go back to our friends or family, the people we are familiar with, and we think we can pick those relationships up right where we left off. But once we have experienced trauma and are dealing with significant losses, relationships change. We don't trust as we once did, and we no longer see ourselves as safe as we once did. This limits who we are in these relationships.

When relationships break down, community breaks down. And when community breaks down, we find ourselves unable to collaborate or work well with other people. We no longer feel comfortable having conversations as we once did. This diminishes our sense of self, a sense of agency or empowerment to change things and move forward. Sadly, many churches and Christian institutions are so trauma uninformed and trauma insensitive that they think their culture is healthy and safe for all people. Those in the trauma zone know better. The six pillars of a trauma-safe culture are designed to heal us and protect us from these losses and so create a trauma-free space. Trauma-informed care is an approach that seeks to promote safety within an organization, system, or program. A trauma-informed approach assumes that each individual we interact with may have experienced trauma in the past. Notice that word *assumes*. One of the goals of a trauma-safe environment is to avoid retraumatization. Trauma-informed care works from the understanding that we've all experienced adversity, though it also recognizes we have not all been traumatized by adversity. Because we don't know what others have experienced, we need to create a safe space, and a safe space is formed by healthy boundaries.[2]

Boundaries in Relationships

It is impossible to talk about trauma care without doing a deep dive into the boundaries that protect our safety. Being trauma informed starts with safety because trauma takes away our safety. Even if the trauma is only perceived trauma, perceived trauma still sits in our bodies and takes away our perception of our safety. Safety matters to churches and ministries because it is something we create. We create safety within our relationships—with ourselves and within our staff—before we can offer it to others. Relational boundaries are necessary.

Boundaries are expressed (or not) "expectations and needs that help you feel safe and comfortable in your relationships."[3] God designed us to form relationships with others, and because God designed us this way, we all desire relationships and closeness with other people. Yet we often don't know how to go about forming relationships in the healthiest of ways. Instead, we learn through breakdowns and difficulties that relationships are hard, they can get ugly, and they can cause deep pain. Connection with others is difficult because we fail to identify or communicate boundaries, and a lack of boundaries creates unsafe and unhealthy relationships. On the flip side, clarifying what one expects in a relationship, clarifying its boundaries, can help create safe and healthy relationships.

Healthy boundaries prevent us from morphing into the other person. They let me stay me and you stay you. Whether pastors, congregants, or those serving others in ministry, boundaries help us become friendly, but not necessarily friends. (More about this later.) Boundaries give us a clearer understanding of our limits and responsibilities as leaders in professional relationships. They also help those being served to better understand limits and responsibilities. The formation of healthy boundaries helps everyone feel safe without limiting anyone's potential.

All of this raises the question, "Why?" Boundaries help us connect and be with another individual while not losing our identity in the other individual. Our goal is to be helpful for the people we minister to or serve without limiting their potential—or our own boundaries. Let's consider the diagram in figure 1, which illustrates the Zone of Helpfulness.

Boundaries enable us to remain in the Zone of Helpfulness when we are caring for someone. We create complications in a relationship when we move too far right or left, when we merge too much with the other person (overinvolved) or when we become a disinterested "helper" (underinvolved). Let's look at some examples of what each of these might look like in a helping relationship.

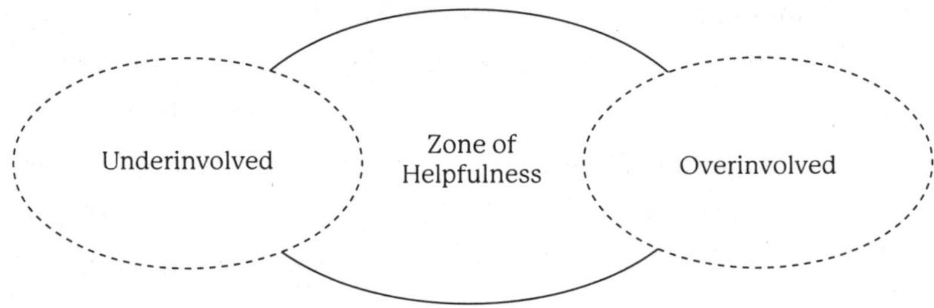

Figure 1: The Zone of Helpfulness

When I (Adrienne) offer to help someone, I might throw out some ideas for what a person needs to do. If I notice that the person who is listening to these ideas seems to like them and agree with them but does not follow through with them, I am faced with a decision. I can explore with them why they are unable to move forward. I could also take on some of the work myself and do it for them. When I do for someone what only they can do for themselves, I cheat them out of that experience of problem-solving or sacrificing or managing their time. And at that point I have moved into the circle of being overinvolved. There are always times when we can do something for someone to help them, even if they could do it themselves. But the key is that we do not want to make someone dependent on us. We may like how it feels to help someone, and many helpers are tempted to be overinvolved because of this. We like to be needed or we like to be the person who rescues someone. But when we become overinvolved, we communicate that the one we are caring for is dependent on us. In addition, the over-involved form of relationship means that person will have to live with the consequences of what we decide for them.

On the other end of the spectrum, underinvolved, is what happens when we have too much on our plates or are feeling burned out or overwhelmed, and we don't offer the suggestions those we care for need so that they can resolve an issue. This happens when ministries are short staffed or when people show up and need us to do everything for them (and we refuse). It may happen that some people are overinvolved with some people, while underinvolved with others. We stay minimally available to remain within the Zone of Helpfulness, but there is just not enough of us to go around.

But when we protect our time by expressing clear boundaries—what and whom we will take on and when—we can better serve those we are called to serve. Staying in the middle of the Zone of Helpfulness helps individuals avoid compassion fatigue because they are neither too involved or underinvolved: "Appropriate boundaries actually increase our ability to care about others."[4] When we move too far from the zone, we are indulging in meeting our own needs more than serving others. If I need to be needed and this person helps meet that need, my need has become central. My work becomes about meeting my needs and not the person in need of help. Or if I am burned out and overworked when someone comes to me and needs help, I am also meeting my need first by being underinvolved. To be clear, I am not saying we should not think about our own needs. On the contrary, we should think first about our needs before we seek to help others with their needs, and set clear boundaries. Then when we are meeting someone else's needs, we can communicate those boundaries in a way that is not meeting our own needs at the cost of the other person. People who are in caring relationships need to learn not to use people for their own gain or satisfaction. If we are not careful, our caring relationship can flip into one in which the one we are caring for starts caring for us instead. This is called role reversal, and it is not healthy.

Friendly Without Being Friends

Earlier, we made a statement about being friendly, but not friends. Being on staff in a church or ministry and having a role or job in which we regularly interact with congregants or other individuals we minister to is different from friendship. We provide spiritual teaching and spiritual and emotional support to these individuals. We receive training and support to be effective in providing this teaching and support. Let's consider three different aspects of this type of relationship and why it is different from friendship.

First, let's say you work at a church, organization, or institution where, in your perception, the relationships between staff, administration, and faculty lack boundaries. You perceive that a genuinely caring relationship, which is standard Christian behavior, has become something different. Perhaps it is a therapeutic relationship or even a very close friend-to-friend relationship. Such relationships have gone too far when codependency forms. This can happen when one person becomes a therapist to another, when the relationship becomes friend to friend and complicates the professional role at the organization, or when the relationship between two people interferes with their professional responsibilities.

Friendships among individuals with a power differential can also become complicated and messy. Most friendships at work among staff are fine because they are on an even playing field. Friendships among congregants are also on an even playing field and hopefully will happen. But when bosses try to be friends with those they employ or pastors have friends among their congregants, these relationships can become complicated and hard to manage, especially if one individual's position oversees the other's. When the friendship tries to operate on an even playing field—the congregant giving spiritual advice to a pastor or the employee being there emotionally for the boss (which does happen)—this creates a dynamic that both individuals sense as complicated. This also explains why many pastors feel so lonely. They try to have friends at church but realize the people they thought were friends really just wanted care from their pastor. Congregants generally don't understand how to be there for their pastors or how to take care of them in a healthy way.

There are three aspects of the relationship between a minister or ministry professional and a congregant or someone being served. The first is care and trust. The care and trust in this relationship typically starts out focused on the individual in need of care. The staff understands the challenges and emotions of being human and being Christian in relationships. This caring and trusting relationship hopefully builds trust and commitment from the individual being served. When care and trust are seen and felt from the served individual, this is often shared back to the pastor or professional. The relationship can then become a mutually caring and trusting relationship, even if the power differential is still present. However, a healthy, boundaried relationship can also work, even if it does not become truly mutual. If a pastor cares for and builds a trusting relationship with an individual in their church, and this person struggles to fully care about the pastor or trust them, they can still depend on and seek help from the pastor. Not every relationship should be mutual.

The second aspect of the relationship to consider is its focus. The focus should not be mutual, meaning the focus of the individual being served is a self-directed focus. When the caring person is speaking with the cared-for, where do we want the focus of the cared-for to be? We want their focus to be on themselves. We want them to be thinking of what is happening for them. Why are they feeling this way? What have they done for themselves so far? The caring person, on the other hand, should be other-focused. The caring person's focus should be on the cared-for. The caring person should not be focused on himself or herself, trying to get their needs met by making sure they are heard or heeded, or by making sure their feelings are taken into account. To put this into a church context, pastors and ministry professionals are other-focused when caring for individuals. The relationship between the caring person and the cared-for—between the pastor and his or her congregant—is not mutual in focus.

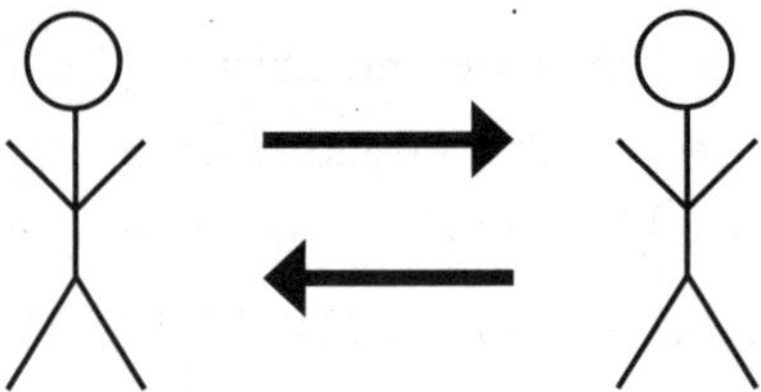

Figure 2: Care and Trust

The third aspect of this relationship to consider is perspective. Another word for perspective is point of view. For the cared-for, the perspective is internal. They will see things through their point of view or lens, and that is what the caring person wants to understand. The caring person doesn't want to see the cared-for's problem or life

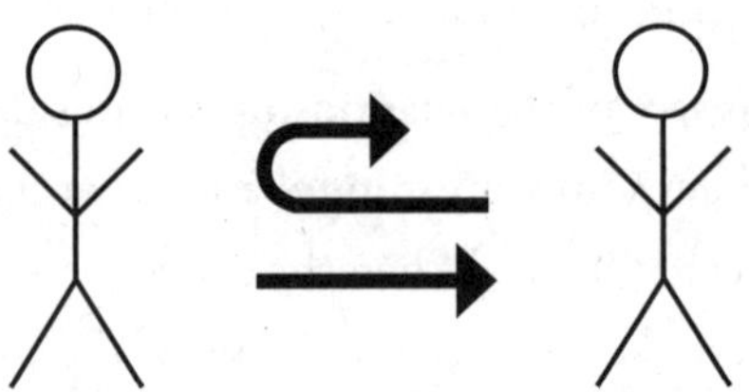

Figure 3: Focus

through the caring person's eyes. They want to see the problem through the cared-for person's eyes. The cared-for person's perspective should be internal, while the caring person has an external perspective. The caring person's aim is to understand the cared-for person. Again, this relationship is not mutual in perspective.

Notice that all three aspects of the relationship are about whose needs are being served. Who came to help whom? Who came needing help? Boundaries enable the appropriate relationship to form care and trust while maintaining the focus and perspective on the individual who is being served. This is not a relationship where the pastor or professional gets their own needs met. And that is why we can say this relationship is not a friendship relationship.

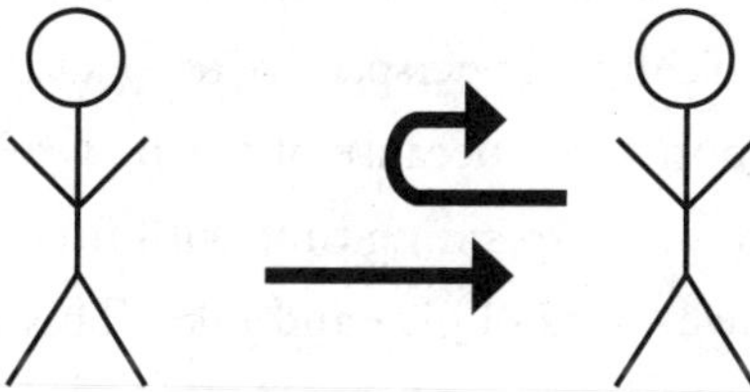

Figure 4: Perspective

When we are in a friendship with someone and there is no power differential, everything is mutual. We meet the other's needs and also get our needs met. This is why a friendship functions differently from a caring pastoral relationship or a professional relationship in the workplace. Most relationships at work that are called friendships are not genuine friendship relationships because they are not mutual. Aristotle famously distinguished three kinds of friends, though he indicated that only the third is a genuine friendship. We have friendships of (1) utility, (2) pleasure, and (3) virtue.[5] In today's professional world, most of us have relationships of utility: I do this task for you, and you do this task for me. We may also form pleasure relationships in our workplace. For example, I like to binge-watch a TV show and so do you, and we share this common pleasure and chat about it in the lunchroom. The first two relationships can exist either in a hierarchy (a worker and a boss) or between mutuals (two coworkers). The third category of relationship, virtue relationships, are more intense, personal, and necessarily mutual, and they take more time and energy. In these, we know one another, we share everything with one another, and we mutually provide insight into the development of one another's character. Most friendship relationships at work fall in either the first or second categories, but if a workplace relationship involves this third aspect of virtue, the professional relationship may be compromised.

So what happens when our boundaries get blurred or when we realize that we never even identified or communicated boundaries with another person? Typically, our perspective or focus gets distorted. This distortion occurs most often because of the power differential in our relationship. When we are spending time with friends, there is mutual focus and perspective—lots of give and take. This is easy to manage and feels healthy to us because we are on an equal playing field with the other person. We should not feel a power differential inside a true friendship. But when there is a power differential—like that between a pastor and a congregant, a professor and a student, or a boss and a worker—the relationship is not mutual and thus is not a true friendship. It is, in the best sense of the word, professional. Always remember, the one with more power will at times need to assert that power to maintain it and even to protect it. The person with less power then becomes vulnerable to the one with power.

In caring and cared-for relationships, then, the two individuals are operating differently. The cared-for comes from a place of need, and the caring person comes from a place of care. The caring person is in the position of influence. The caring person is being trusted, willingly, and they need to work at being trustworthy.

Self-Care Required

Those who are in a position to care for others also need to be self-aware. The person with power in the relationship may need to engage in self-care or healing work. This includes pastors and those in ministry, but also moms and dads, really anyone in a position of caring for another. We all need to know ourselves and know our pain or hurts. When we know ourselves and are aware of our needs, we are less likely to use other people to meet those needs. We should develop an awareness of our own annoyances, our own shortcomings, and where we tend to become overinvolved. We take care of ourselves to be more available to take care of others. Doing our own self-work enables us to foster safe and healthy connections with others. More can be said about this, but there are several great resources available that can help you become more self-aware and emotionally healthy as an individual. Two recommended resources are *Trauma Stewardship: An Everyday Guide to Caring for Self While Caring for Others* by Laura van Dernoot Lipsky and Connie Burk, and *Why Emotions Matter* by Tristen Collins and Jonathan Collins.

In summary, the first two pillars for cultivating a trauma-safe institution are safety and boundaries, and as you can see, they are closely related to one another. We now turn to the third pillar, which is also closely connected. Healthy, trauma-safe institutions cultivate trust.

Chapter 11

Trust and Transparency

I (Adrienne) once attended a church where the pastors' wives met monthly for dinner. Because I was a pastor's wife, I attended these dinners. I was young, and at first these dinners were beautiful and life-giving. However, over time, as I was growing in my profession as a counselor, I saw the dinners in a different light. I remember one night showing up to the monthly dinner and immediately the discussion turned to recent statements made by another woman who was employed at the church. She had shared—privately with the pastors—that she had been having a sexual relationship with a former pastor of the church, someone who had left and was now working at another church in our area. According to this woman, the sexual relationship had begun while she was seeing this pastor for counseling about her marriage, which ultimately ended in a divorce. Our church obviously had questions about this disclosure, so she had sat down with the current senior pastor and executive pastor to answer their detailed questions about the relationship. All of this information was apparently documented, and it was this documentation of the sexual relationship that the women at our dinner were asking me about: Had I read her statements? Had I read the intimate details of when and how often they had sex?

I sat there with these women throughout the dinner as they spoke about what this woman had disclosed privately to the pastors, and I kept thinking to myself, "This is not right, this is not right, we have not been invited into this woman's life and story!" What benefit was it to the church for us to know these details? And did it really benefit us to sit around a dinner table and discuss them?

When I returned home later that evening, my question was more introspective: Why did this bother me so much? In my counseling work, I hear stories of abuse and sexual encounters with their intimate details regularly. Yet in this case my body was communicating to me that something was not right. And I realized that I was especially bothered by these women having access to this information. The woman's disclosure to the pastors was not intended to be widely shared. She had been asked to disclose the nature of her relationship with the former pastor, and she did—to the new pastor and the executive pastor. But she did not disclose this information to those men's wives, and she did not share this personal information about herself with anyone else. Had the men, prior to her disclosure, told her that they were going to let their wives read her statement? Was she informed how easy it would be for some individuals to learn her story? The answer is clearly no. At the dinner, I had been offered the opportunity to read her statement, and I had turned it down.

There are many implications we can draw from this story, but I want to focus our attention on the matter of trust, particularly in light of the Bible's severe words about the destructive power of gossip and slander. Jesus once said, "For out of the heart come evil thoughts—murder, adultery, sexual immorality, theft, false testimony, slander" (Matt. 15:19 NIV). Paul feared that in Corinth the following sins would be visible: "I fear that there may be discord, jealousy, fits of rage, selfish ambition, slander, gossip, arrogance and disorder" (2 Cor. 12:20 NIV). James, the brother of Jesus, wrote, "Brothers and sisters, do not slander one another. Anyone who speaks against a brother or sister or judges them speaks against the law and judges it" (James 4:11 NIV). Peter wrote to his churches, "Rid yourselves of all malice and all deceit, hypocrisy, envy, and slander of every kind" (1 Peter 2:1 NIV). That word "slander" shows up repeatedly among lists of sins that are destructive to the church. It translates the Greek term *katalalia*, which means to speak against someone in a way that degrades and devalues the person. I'm convinced that the dinner conversation that night was an instance of slander and harmed the reputation of that woman. We can put such a conversation into perspective if we simply ask ourselves whether we would talk like that if the woman were in the room or if the woman would find out what was said about her. Following the Golden Rule of Jesus, as a boundary for discussions, would have reshaped the entire conversation.

The decisions we make about handling sensitive information that we have been entrusted with can either build or destroy trust. My takeaway from that meeting was that everyone who shares private information with the senior or executive pastor at this church is also sharing it with their wives—and perhaps all of the pastors' wives. In my experience, this information was readily shared among them all. Once information like that becomes widely known, any trust in handling personally disclosed information will be gone. In this case, the executive pastor handled all conflict among church members and church staff. Did the employees know that some of these pastors were sharing information with their wives? The fact that this private information was a dinner conversation among them reveals an unhealthy pattern.

Some workplaces have private chats in which people share information about one another. But what happens when a coworker, through an accidental leak of a private chat about her, suddenly discovers that others have been talking about her? What happens when a culture becomes full of "secrets"? What do we say when someone says to us, "I want to tell you about someone here, but I need you to hold it in confidence"? Without laying down a bunch of unenforceable rules, we need to step back and ask whether a toxic culture has formed. The person who discovers that secrets about her are being shared by others will experience shame and betrayal and will sense that this place is unsafe.

Because this is my (Adrienne) background, I want to share some insights from the world of professional therapy as a helpful starting point in our discussion. First, there is the clear expectation that whatever is disclosed to the therapist stays with the therapist. There are exceptions to this rule, of course, but we'll cover those later. In general, those who care for others need to discipline themselves to protect the trust and confidence placed in them. If this is expected of therapists, we must expect it as well of those who care for others in church settings and Christian institutions. Step one in developing a culture of trust is silencing secret communication and becoming transparent with those we serve.

The Assumption in the Middle of the Room

The next step in building trustworthiness and transparency is having an agreed upon policy of what information is shared and who it is shared with. One might assume that the onus is on the person sharing to ask about this before they share. But I would argue that most people are naturally going to trust their spiritual leaders and assume that the information they share with them will be shared with others only if it is in their best interests. The oft-unspoken assumption in these disclosures to church leaders is that what is shared will not be broadcast to others: What I tell you stays with you. We also need to ask, What would the disclosing person want to be known? In whose best interest is it to share this information? Does sharing information benefit, or more likely hurt, the church or ministry in some way? There can be no trust without transparency, and transparency begins before a person discloses the information. Transparency means all parties in the conversation know their boundaries.

When we do not have policies or procedures regarding disclosure of private information that can be shared with everyone within an organization or a congregation, we create an unsafe environment, one that erodes trust. Violation of these policies is also a violation of boundaries and safety, our first two pillars. And when people experience trauma and are led to believe the world is no longer a safe place, they lose trust in the safety and goodness of the world. Trust is core to all relationships and a cornerstone of Christian community. Safety, the guiding principle in forming a trauma-informed and trauma-sensitive Christian culture, is built on the foundation of trust and transparency. Many organizations and ministries think of themselves as trustworthy because they are telling the truth and work not to lie or deceive others. But trust is more than just telling the truth. Trust includes being a responsible deposit of personal, private, and shame-evoking information.

When an individual shares personal information, that person puts themselves at risk in sharing with another. The disclosing person is trusting the one to whom they speak, and trust is held when the information remains in confidence, when privacy and respect are honored and maintained. They can share something with a caring individual and know that information is guarded. Transparency is simply being open and upfront about one's personal information. If we want to build trust, we need to have an honest conversation about boundaries with the person we are caring for before we disclose sensitive information. Some persons may be surprised to learn with whom their personal information will or will not be shared. But through the promises made in this transparent moment, the disclosing person will learn how their personal information is kept private and see the boundaries that are in place to protect them. They will know that the information is theirs and is protected, not something to be tossed around without much thought. When a disclosing person is brought into the conversation with promises, they are granted some measure of authority and agency over the intimate details they share. That authority lays the groundwork for them to build their esteem, their agency, and their voice. They recognize that trustworthiness is a priority and a privilege. This is something trauma-informed organizations and ministries can give back to the traumatized, who have often lost trust through the wounds they have experienced.

Trust Pillar, Boundary Pillar

Learning to trust again can happen over time, and many times a person may be unaware that their trust is growing. The person with whom they are sharing or communicating may say or do something that reveals how much the disclosing person trusts them, which in turn promotes the person's ability to trust. But when trust is broken or even threatened, it turns the world upside down. The world quickly becomes systemically untrustworthy. A person no longer knows which way is up and is no longer sure he or she can trust anyone or anything ever again. Trust is difficult to rebuild once broken, and trauma in the form of abuse often leaves a victim unable to trust themselves or others. If grooming is what led to the trauma, they may have had an experience in which they placed their trust in an abuser. Now that this trust has been broken by abuse, they look around and wonder whether they can trust anyone ever again.

The pillar of good boundaries will nurture a culture that is safe, and this creates an environment where people can trust others. Those caring for others can help an individual to grow, but the helper needs to be worthy of trust. So how do we develop this ability to be worthy of others' trust? We can define boundaries and then transparently communicate them to the person being helped. Remember that transparent boundaries are clearly established limits placed on the relationship. These allow for predictability and confidence to grow in the relationship.

Transparent boundaries, in turn, nurture trustworthy relationships. If someone comes into my (Adrienne) office to work with me, my role is clearly defined as the counselor and their role as the client. I do not assume each party knows their role; we talk through these role definitions. I let them know what they can expect of me and from me as their counselor. This means also letting them know what they should not expect of and from me. I also communicate to them what it means for their role as a client, and then we dialogue about these roles and expectations. Is this what they are looking for? Do these roles make sense to them? Is this still the type of relationship they want to enter into? I realize having such a conversation isn't terribly organic, and some people push against that. But it isn't organic for a reason. There is a power differential in our relationship, and the person who holds more power needs to be aware of this and communicate that difference to the person who holds less power. The person in authority needs to protect the person with less authority. The first way to do so is to make sure everyone understands the relationship and its boundaries. Even if having a conversation about that does not feel organic or natural, in the end people are better off when they know and understand the expectations, especially at the beginning of a new relationship. I (Adrienne) do what I can to empower a client with agency so they know they can trust me, and I do what I can to assure the client I am trustworthy.

Leaders and Roles

Leaders in a church or ministry organization, and this broadly includes all levels of ministry, have certain roles and responsibilities. Some of these are little more than expectations people assume about that role. Some of these expectations confuse those who have caring responsibilities, and they need to be clearly communicated. For example, when is the caring person available to meet or talk? Should the cared-for text the person in the middle of the night? If the caring person wakes up and responds, they communicate constant availability. The same is true in responding to emails. Does the caring person hit the return email after work hours because they have a free moment? In writing this, one of our spouses reminded us that if we respond to emails or text messages immediately, we set up an expectation that we will always respond immediately. We recommend that the caring person communicate boundaries about their availability. I (Scot) am old enough to remember a time when work hours were actually work hours. It was a time before the internet and email, when I typed letters and then corrected them and retyped them, when my office phone was in my school office and my home phone was in my home, when colleagues did not do business on the home phone—when I was home, I was home and not at work. There was a clear boundary between my home life and my work life.

Today, this is all in the rearview mirror, but what we see in that rearview mirror was far better than the boundaryless world in which we now live. Since those boundaries may not exist any longer, we need to set boundaries, and those are best communicated early in the relationship. Parameters can also include what the caring person is required to disclose to state agencies or law enforcement. For example, if the caring person is considered a mandated reporter, people need to know that they have a legal obligation to disclose child abuse or potential harm to another individual. As a counselor, I (Adrienne) am clear with every adult and child who enters my office that I must report some types of information and may have to violate client confidentiality if they tell me they know of a child being abused or if they are going to harm another individual. I don't tell them after they have made the disclosure; I let them know about this at the beginning of the relationship.

Recently, a commenter on my (Scot) Substack wanted me to become his friend, entering into a daily interactive relationship in which I would read his Substack entries and write my comments to him. He shared with me what he wanted me to do. But I didn't want to. He huffed and puffed and eventually went away, but I saw this as healthy boundary maintenance. (So did my wife, Kris, by the way.) It is not uncommon to have this sort of commenter on a Substack or social media platform. Some people have unrealistic expectations of what they can require from me and what I am able to give them. Clear boundaries matter. Even though it was not the answer this person wanted to hear, by being transparent with him, I modeled this pillar with him.

Another important boundary that can help form trust involves a leader communicating what she is and is not equipped to handle. When the cared-for needs help with something that is beyond a leader's expertise or even confidence, the caring person openly and honestly explains where the person in need can pursue next steps. Perhaps it is a pastor directing the person to speak with someone at the church who specializes in handling trauma or conflict. Or it may be a referral to a clinic or a professional in another organization. Boundaries not only protect the relationship, they build trust that this individual is looking out for the cared-for's best interests. By clarifying their limits, a caring person communicates that they are human and limited, but also that they truly want the best for the other person, even knowing when they cannot offer it. This is healthy and refreshing because we are all human and have limits. It demonstrates that the caring person knows herself and that she does not expect too much from herself. Furthermore, clarifying limits communicates that we all need other people and that we do not walk this journey of caring for others alone.

Finally, in creating a relationship that is trustworthy, the caring person clarifies transparency about any personal information disclosed by the cared-for person. What happens if the caring person needs to disclose any of the information shared? Will the caring person talk to the cared-for first? Or afterward? Or will it be a dialogue? A person who needs help and who does not know how to trust or does not know that they are not fully capable of trust will not always be the one who thinks of asking these questions. They are usually not aware of what they need to know. Many hurt and traumatized individuals will not feel the freedom or safety to openly ask for what they need, if they know what they need. A person in the trauma zone may desire to trust someone again but, because of past church wounds, may be hesitant to trust a pastor or a church leader. The caring person who is seeking to establish trust will communicate to the cared-for what this relationship means and what will and will not be done with the information disclosed.

Let's return to the story I shared at the opening of this chapter. The pastors in this situation should have been up-front that they had a practice of sharing any personal details revealed to them with their wives as well. Even better, they should have established with their wives a clear professional boundary that because of the nature of their work, they would not be able to share private information with their spouses.

If they felt it was necessary to share this personal information with other pastors or ministry workers, they also needed to think about the problems with not letting the woman know about this. By not being transparent and admitting their potential disclosures, they violated all three of our pillars and failed to nurture trust, healthy boundaries, and a place of safety in their church culture.

These pastors may not have even considered this, but by stewarding private information responsibly and transparently, they could have nurtured trust among their coworkers as well. And when leaders set clear boundaries and expectations for what is shared and not shared, a culture of transparency develops and we see greater mutuality between people. Staff will follow their leaders' example and show trust and transparency to the people they are caring for. When these practices and boundaries are encouraged from the top down, it can have a ripple effect through every level of a church or ministry organization. Which leads us to our fourth pillar of a trauma-informed culture: mutuality.

Chapter 12

Mutuality

We tend to grow most when in proximity to significant others. People challenge us in the best of ways, and also in the worst of ways. In relationship we are known and come to know ourselves. Experts speak of humans as dyadic: We become who we are because of others to whom we relate.[1] We are dyadic in relationship to our mothers or fathers, to siblings, to friends, to those in our churches, and to those in our workplaces. Dyadic personality theory counters a monadic approach, the theory that we stand alone and function alone and know ourselves entirely on our own.

Modernity has tended to make us think we are monadic when really we are dyadic. Furthermore, as we learn to relate to other people, we better learn how to relate to the dyad of all dyadic relationships: God. If we cannot grow in our relationship with the people around us, how can we learn to be in relationship with our creator? Being in relationship is essential to human development. Staying in relationship and working through challenges creates stronger social skills and bonds. And while relationships are not easy, they are necessary for anyone who wants to grow in interpersonal skills. But here is the tragic mic drop: Trauma disrupts our ability to form social bonds and remain in relationship. Trauma leads us to go it alone, baiting us to think we can live monadically, disconnected from others.

Trauma Disconnects

Trauma leaves us feeling isolated and alone. Someone in the trauma zone questions whether others can understand what they have been through. Trauma isolates a person into thinking they are the only one, that they are one of a kind in their experience. Peer support is helpful in combatting this because it brings us into relationships with others who have had similar experiences. As we have seen, whenever there is a loss of safety or trust in a relationship, it disrupts our ability to feel safe with others and to trust others.

The fourth pillar of a trauma-safe environment attempts to level the playing field as it invites us into mutual relationships. Safety and trust are integral in relationships, but so many of the relationships that we have been talking about have a power dynamic connected to them. A person in need of care goes to a pastor or director or administrator who is seen as a helper or professional. The person in the trauma zone becomes acutely and immediately aware of the power dynamic present, even when the one with power does not recognize it. (Which is a problem, because those in the trauma zone wonder whether every person to whom they speak could become an abuser or rewound them.) In these situations, it is normal for someone in the trauma zone to be wary and to struggle to trust the one who holds the power. Peer support is an alternative to this, offering mutuality, a peer-to-peer connection. It offers what is missing in these other relationships, the secret ingredient to genuine friendship: mutuality and equality. Peer support is a way of redressing the imbalance of power.

Mutuality Connects

Mutual support connects people. A few years ago, I (Scot) was invited to speak at Restore, a conference started by Julie Roys of *The Roys Report*.[2] Julie, formerly a radio personality at Moody Radio's well-known Christian station in the Chicago area (WMBI), has worked in recent years to expose corruption as she seeks to bring redemptive goodness to churches. Kris and I both attended the conference, and what surprised us most was the fellowship between those who had experienced abuse, silencing, gift degradation, and oppression in churches. These people clearly needed one another and benefited from knowing each other. Hearing the stories of others provided them with a common language. Getting to know peers with similar experiences helped them to know themselves more. My time there showed me the power of mutuality to help people heal from abuse.

Mutual relationship acknowledges the feelings of helplessness and worthlessness that traumatized individuals experience, their sense that they have nothing to offer the world. But what does this kind of peer support look like in a church? Peer-to-peer support is often found around a table at a Bible study or when volunteers serve together and realize they have similar stories. It can look like a mentoring or discipleship relationship. Do we have avenues in our churches and ministries where people can show up and get to know each other? Are the groups where people meet hierarchical with a power dynamic at work? People within a congregation or ministry need space to form mutual bonds and make connections. And again, this needs to be modeled by leaders. If community and relationships are important to the pastor, the ministry professionals, and the elders and leaders, they should seek to build a structured environment where mutual relationships can flourish.

Sibling Relationships

In his letters to the church in Corinth, Paul uses brother and sister language nearly fifty times. Here's one example: "I appeal to you, brothers and sisters" (1 Cor. 1:10 NIV). What is often ignored is that Paul's favorite language for the church is not of church but of siblings, and his favorite image for the relationships between Christians flows from family relationships. The church can become the environment where close bonds grow and flourish because the church is a new family living together as a new community. When church is a family, people are not alone, attempting to struggle through life as monads. Families live life together; family relationships exhibit dyadic relationships. Siblings talk about what matters most to them. They share day-to-day activities, chores, and responsibilities with one another. They depend on one another and share in meeting one another's needs.

Close attachments and healthy relationships take time. But time alone isn't the way to develop these relationships. Programs at a church can take time and still never lead to peer-to-peer relationships. Have you ever been in a Bible study or a small group class at church, spending lots of time learning information or sharing and interacting with the leader, but not the other group members? People who start attending a church are often encouraged to participate in more programs and meetings or to volunteer to support other programs. The assumption is that these programs and meetings will naturally build community, and that may happen. But we still need to ask whether we're building the kind of community that feels like family. "Family-making" in a church is what experts call "fictive"—a metaphor for the realities of fellowship. Fictive family-making takes both time and connection, connection that requires safety, trust, and healthy boundaries. Mutuality becomes part of the process of family-making. Gabor Maté, a well-known physician who specializes in childhood development, writes about these connections, saying that safety is about more than avoiding threats; it is the presence of emotional attunement within a relationship.[3] Emotional attunement is often what we are looking for in close family-style relationships. Emotional attunement leads us to the feeling of safety. Safety then allows us to enter into relationships, to know and be known. Finding and making friends or community often depends on our ability to attune to others. This is a development that takes time. Churches would benefit from creating and encouraging spaces solely to provide time and space to attune to others, to get to know our church siblings.

Small groups can be a vital organ in forming healthy, growing, and nurturing churches. In some churches, leaders want to shape and even control what happens in small groups that meet in homes during the week. But different people have different hopes for what happens in a small group. Healthy churches encourage small groups to become what they need to become. Kris and I (Scot) have been in a small group for several years. The group decided at the outset that it would not be a Bible study or a group that had assignments to read to prepare for each gathering. Instead, we spent our time hearing each person's story, catching up with one another's stories each gathering, and praying together. We read a compline prayer to end our sessions.

Over time the group has changed as some have come and gone. Kris and I find that we miss those who have left. They were, as Kris often says, part of our "support group." Three of the couples who have left get together each year to catch up with one another, and they'd love to get together more often! The relationships of those who have been in this small group became sibling relationships, and sibling relationships are rooted in trust. As we will see in the final chapter, when churches or institutions go through troubled times with fractured relationships, sibling trust either breaks down or sustains them to carry on. Churches that don't have widespread sibling relationships are the most easily fractured. Churches that permit small groups to become divisive are also easily fractured, and restoring trust after fractures can be one of a church's biggest challenges. To return to the apostle Paul, not only were the sibling relationships at Corinth in tension but Paul himself was having a hard time trusting himself to them as a sibling, and they had the same problem with him. When sibling relationships break down, we get 2 Corinthians 10–13, and that's why we examined those chapters as we did. They can be a mirror to our own sibling relationships.

Mutuality and Healing

As we've seen, a fundamental relationship for a person in the trauma zone is with a caring person, often a therapist or other professional. However, it often happens that a person in the trauma zone, while in the company of a caring other, senses they are not the only one who has felt this way or has experienced something painful. This may be why Paul retreated so often to Ephesus. He felt safe there, and he had brothers and sisters in Christ who knew and understood his experiences. That mutual, sibling relationship likely contributed to a sense of safety, growing trust, connection, and attunement for Paul.

Some individuals will feel safer in peer relationships. Finding and forming those relationships helps them grow in connection with others. Why? Because painful experiences are normalized and validated when they are shared mutually with a peer. When the connection takes place with someone who has experienced something similar, the validation they experience is even more powerful than what they can get from a professional helper or leader. They are validated by someone who has walked in their shoes. This is why some trauma survivors first learn to trust peers in these mutual relationships before they can fully trust someone with power over them.

In a mutual relationship, both persons grow. The person receiving help and support, in experiencing care and empathy, discovers safety, trust, and mutuality. Their confidence in relationships expands, giving them courage to risk trusting others. The caring person leaves with a sense of pride and fulfillment, expressed in acts of love toward another, that they were able to offer support to someone who needed it. The caring person is empowered because they find that their story matters to others, that they can actually help others. In mutual relationships of people who have experienced trauma, the victim of trauma is able to offer a gift of support to someone else who is on a similar journey.

Let us not forget that God is also present when we are caring for others. The love of that caring person expresses God's love, and the cared-for person who experiences this love experiences God's love. God's love and our shared love creates a circle of loving care. Here I am reminded of Paul's words to the Corinthians. A literal translation reveals this mutuality in Paul, and I'll number the various elements to show how Paul sees this circling of care for one another: "Blessed is the God and Father of our Lord Yēsous Christos, the Father of sympathies and God of all encouragement, (1) the one encouraging us in all our trouble (2) so we might be able to encourage the ones in all trouble (3) through the encouragement, in which we ourselves are encouraged by God" (2 Cor. 1:3–4 *Second Testament*). As Paul states, it all begins with God. Then we experience God's encouragement. We pass God's encouragement on to others. And finally, we realize that the encouragement we pass on is God's encouragement.

Organic Mutuality Surpasses Programs Embodying Power

I (Adrienne) grew up in a megachurch in Arizona and have memories of strong peer support and mutual relationships. Many teens are desperately looking for love, caring relationships, and genuine mutuality, and we should not minimize that need, because it expresses how God has designed us. It's especially strong among teenagers.

The youth group at this church was large and thriving, and we had a large number of young, volunteer small-group leaders. They had good programs that brought in the numbers the church wanted. But outside of these programs, the staff leaders really lived life with us as students. They would take us out to lunch. They would drive us to the gas station for sodas. They had a million sleepovers and game nights. So while there were programs for small-group Bible studies and classes, and these were good and helpful, the healthy sibling relationships we had really grew outside of these programs.

Our small group leaders worked to create an environment for us to flourish in sibling relationships with one another as students as well. We spent time with our leaders in this trusting, safe environment of mutuality and were able to share our similar strengths and struggles as students. We were brought together to share our lives, and many of us did. What may be unique about this environment was both our age and our desire for mutuality, for genuine Christian siblingship. Many of these relationships formed spontaneously, organically, and adjusted themselves to what we needed in the moment.

Fast-forward twenty years and I found myself in another group—this one for young moms. Again, we were at similar ages and similar life stages, but now it felt almost impossible to get these women together outside of the scheduled programs and classes. We all attended that monthly get-together, though, sharing a meal together and talking about the message presented. We would also talk about being lonely and cooped up in our homes with no adults to talk to all day, just little children who needed us but wouldn't listen to us. So the leaders scheduled more outside activities, planned events, organized park play dates, scheduled dinners out. Sadly, no one attended these extra outings. We were surrounded by people who knew and felt exactly what it was like to be a mom to young children. We could have experienced support and encouragement. We could have basked in refreshment of the soul. But it didn't take place. Why? Because these events were "created" by a church that modeled connections and relationships through programs and classes.

In one church setting (the latter), the leadership set up the events, decided what would be done, and told us when it would happen. There was no colaboring or sharing of responsibility. These events were neither organic nor spontaneous, and the needs of the moment were not in view. Power was held by a few and not mutually shared, and as a result it was difficult for genuine relationships, healing, and growth to occur. Hierarchy and power tend to work against mutuality and organic relationships. Even at that time, I recognized several moms showing signs of trauma, but because we lacked a network of mutuality, we never formed the relationships needed to move into each other's trauma zones.

The kind of support we needed required collaboration. Collaboration is a form of partnership that nurtures growth and mutual respect. In a relationship of mutuality, a person sees the goodness and positive qualities in other people. They recall and witness their *imago Dei*, that they are image bearers of God. As they work together and serve one another in these mutual relationships, they collaborate with and empower one another. Trauma disconnects people and destroys community, that feeling of belonging. Trauma isolates and detaches us. Trauma survivors struggle to find healthy attachment and belonging because their sense of self-worth has been damaged.

Collaboration restores people from the effects of detachment and isolation. "A collaborative approach is necessary for everyone in an organization or on a campus. In a trauma-informed organization there is an intentional shoulder to shoulder approach and a focus on breaking down hierarchies."[4] Mutuality and collaboration will struggle to form, and often fail, when there is an imbalance of power, and this is true whether it's a mom's group, a small-group Bible study, or a church leadership team. Trauma-informed persons are able to recognize where power dynamics are present but also attune to the misuse and abuse of power.

In her book *Redeeming Power*, author Diane Langberg talks about the abuse of power by highlighting how the leader is the key component to any type of organizational system. This leader often has a close group of followers, and the access this group has to the leader gives them a share of the power from the top. This small group may become very passionate about their mission. However, too often that mission includes holding on to their power. She writes, "It is vital for us to keep in mind that the purpose of any system is for people to stand together to protect, serve, or nurture human beings, who are created in the image of God. . . . The system is for the people; the people do not serve the system."[5] When a group is more focused on holding power than on sharing it to meet people's needs, it is not trauma informed. It is likely both trauma uninformed and trauma unsafe. Mutuality challenges these misuses of power through mutual empowerment.

Trauma survivors long for groups that restore their identity, their sense of being loved, and their ability to form mutual relationships. As Judith Herman writes, "Trauma isolates; the group recreates a sense of belonging. Trauma shames and stigmatizes; the group bears witness and affirms. Trauma degrades the victim; the group exalts her. Trauma dehumanizes the victim; the group restores her humanity. . . . [A]t that moment, the survivor begins to rejoin the human commonality."[6]

Churches often state they have open doors and that everyone is welcome. But are we a welcoming place that communicates and creates a sense of belonging? Does our form of welcoming nurture the pillar of mutuality?

As we develop relationships of mutuality and collaboration, people will feel that they are welcome and belong. They will feel trusted and trustworthy, and they will become trusting people. But we may also need to address imbalances of power that remain. As we will explore in the next chapter, a helpful first step is often letting someone voice their thoughts and opinions, and then letting them know they have been heard. Such empowerment of the person in the trauma zone is the next pillar in creating a trauma-safe culture.

Chapter 13

Empowerment

The fifth pillar of trauma-informed care acknowledges the power differential in helping-healing relationships. This pillar attempts to level the playing field between the caring person and the cared-for person. As it does so, empowerment leans heavily on the pillar of mutuality. Empowerment gives voice, agency, and choice back to the survivor. As Judith Herman writes, "No intervention that takes power away from the survivor can possibly foster her recovery, no matter how much it appears to be in her immediate best interest."[1] We cannot disregard the power differential. Instead, we must validate the victim's experience, which gives them control over themselves, rather than permitting someone else to control them.

In my experience with church leaders who have been credibly accused of inappropriate behavior, whether it was sexual or authoritarian power abuse, empowering someone who claims to be a victim threatens the power and personality of the one being accused. That's why the empowerment of victims is typically threatened from the moment their stories become known. The power is nearly always in the hand of the pastor or leader, and the one with power will often manipulate, verbally abuse, or work in other ways to protect themselves, often in the name of protecting the church's reputation. Because the power is in the hands of that leader and that power can be wielded against them, the victim or whistleblower will sometimes back down. They may even falsely deny there was ever a problem. Herman writes about how a leader might engage in these power manipulations: "In order to escape accountability for his crimes, the perpetrator does everything in his power to promote forgetting. If secrecy fails, the perpetrator attacks the credibility of his victim. If he cannot silence her absolutely, he tries to make sure no one listens."[2] Christian organizations, when facing allegations against the top of their hierarchy, may form false narratives to protect themselves. In the book I (Scot) wrote with my daughter, *A Church called Tov*, I named several false narratives that emerged in the aftermath of devastating news about one leader:[3]

1. Discredit the critics.
2. Demonize the critics.
3. Spin the story.
4. Gaslight the critics.
5. Make the perpetrator the victim (called "DARVO").
6. Silence the truth.
7. Suppress the truth.
8. Issue a fake apology.

The apostle Paul no doubt perceived some of this in his own treatment by the Corinthians. Because power in an organization is so dynamic and its forces are so pervasive, the power dynamic must be recognized as the elephant in the room. It's necessary to flatten the power of the person being accused, and the best way for that to happen is to put the person with power on administrative leave so a review process can take place transparently and with integrity. Those who immediately surrounded the power leader also should be removed from the new circle that seeks to empower the victim so the story can be heard. Only once the accused offender's power is flattened will the victim feel their story might be believed.

Some Practical Points

Empowering victims means caring for victims. This involves working "with" victims and not just doing something "for" them.[4] How are we elevating the voices of the hurt? Trauma survivors should be involved in choosing how much they want to share and who they want to share it with, and they need to be encouraged to share slowly, or at minimum at their own pace, being considerate of their safety.

Not only should victims get to choose how much they share, they should choose how often they tell their stories. Earlier, we shared the story of a female pastor who experienced family trauma while on a mission trip in Latvia. Much of the trauma she experienced occurred after the event that took place in Latvia. It was reexperienced over and over again in the offices of her church when she returned home and returned to work. She was asked to share the incident repeatedly and to talk about the decisions she had made. Rehashing the ordeal caused her to relive the experience again and again. She felt she had no choice but to step back into the situation each time she spoke about it, reliving her trauma. The individuals who questioned her did not stop to ask whether this was helpful or harmful.

There is an organization in Phoenix, Arizona, called Childhelp[5] that cares for children who have witnessed a crime. The guidelines they have implemented have now been adopted by many special victims units across the country. Whenever a woman or child has been the victim of abuse or a sexual crime, the guidelines stipulate that this individual cannot be asked to relive the experience every time an investigator or a lawyer has questions for them. The organization brings in a forensic investigator who gathers the witness statement just one time on camera. The forensic investigator knows exactly what needs to be asked, the correct way to ask questions so the answers can be used in court, and how to ask so the information gathered will be all that everyone needs. The person Childhelp chooses to interview the victim is not a lawyer. Lawyers are trained to defend; forensic investigators are trained to develop curiosity and ask questions.[6] When the investigation is done this way, a victim or witness recounts their story only once.

Unfortunately, not every agency in the country dealing with victims utilizes this approach, and as a result victims have to answer questions related to their abuse multiple times. Sometimes the victim, in deep pain, simply walks away from the process. Doing a well-conducted, onetime interview is one simple way to empower the victim.

Abandonment

Trauma impacts a person's ability to speak up for themselves. They may find they have lost their freedom, agency, and choice. You may wonder how someone can learn to stop speaking up for themselves. In the moment of trauma, the victim may have cried out or asked for help, trying to get someone to pay attention to what was happening, but that plea went unanswered. There may have been no one around to hear the cry. They may have been ignored. They may not have been believed. Regardless, they experienced abandonment, a perception that sets the groundwork for them to believe no one is listening to them or that no one cares about them.

Bruce Perry writes about the ramifications of abandonment on small children in his book *The Boy Who Was Raised as a Dog.* Little children who cry when they are tired, hungry, or lonely and are ignored will eventually stop crying. It is not that they have learned to take care of themselves. Instead, they have learned that having a voice doesn't matter because no one responds. Their voice quiets down, they stop trying to reach out for help and support, and they learn that there is no one around to help them or care for them.[7] The result is that abandoned children slowly learn to do for themselves as best they can. But it is not only children who feel abandoned. A perception of abandonment is widespread among those in the trauma zone.

A caring person will work to restore a person's voice. Having a voice means not just speaking but being heard as well. Our voices give us the ability to reach out to others. Our voices build community and relationships. When we feel seen and heard, we feel safe to engage in friendships. Community keeps us from feeling alone or abandoned. Trauma survivors often feel abandoned. Empowerment reverses abandonment toward safety, trust, and mutual relationships.

A Listening Space

What does this mean for churches and ministry organizations? These organizations should seek to help those who are victims or have experienced trauma to find their voices again. The key practice for implementing this is something we talked about earlier in the book: listening. What victims need most is a listening space, a space in which they know they will be heard. They need to know we want to hear what they have to say and will let them say what needs to be said. Listening well can slow the cycle of abandonment that trauma has set in motion. Listening slowly helps a survivor learn that there are people who care, who hear them, and who want to help them heal. A caring person's listening empowers the cared-for person.

Our brains, when they are flooded, shut down our ability to

communicate. This is one concrete example of how trauma affects us. When our bodies experience a stress arousal response—fight, flight, freeze, or fawn—our whole bodies are pulled into the experience because they have just alerted our brains to go into survival mode. This normal and healthy response affects key areas of our bodies. If there is a threat and we need to survive, our digestive systems shut down because they are not needed at this moment. Our blood pumps a little quicker, our heart rate increases, and our prefrontal cortex goes offline. Our prefrontal cortex houses the language and communication areas of our brains.

This means that when someone is talking about their trauma or is reminded of it, the speech and language centers of their brain are impacted as they think about that traumatic memory.[8] They may lose the ability to know what to say, and they may find themselves unable to put words together or form sentences when speaking about their trauma. Here's the key: The listener needs to be aware of what the body of the cared-for person communicates. The caring person can ask whether the survivor needs a break or would like to take a walk together to get some fresh air. Some people communicate best while walking with others. The responsibility of the caring person is to listen and help the cared-for person make sense of what's happening to them. Crucial moments in the person's story may even be communicated out of order. The person, in their disturbance, may forget important details and then remember them out of order, and that may confuse the listener. But out-of-order storytelling doesn't mean the individual is making something up, nor does it suggest the cared-for person is hiding something. They are still slowly putting the pieces together.

Listening is an art form. I (Scot) am not a therapist, Adrienne is. But I have had numerous people tell me their stories, both in writing and in talking. I have learned that the greater the tension that person is feeling, the more likely it is that I need to ask questions to put the story into an order I can understand. Because my wife, Kris, is a therapist, I have learned a bit more than the average person about the art of asking questions. I have also learned to rehearse the story I hear back to the person to see if they think I understand them. Asking questions so the cared-for person can fill in details and clarify the order of events is a form of listening.

When trauma takes sides in the church or in Christian institutions, the only way forward, and it may be slow and risky and difficult and slow again, is to become listeners. Sometimes what we hear from others may take months to hear well. Sometimes people decide they are appointed to fix things, and fixers often break more things than they fix. Listening, as we said, is an art form, and not everyone is an artist in listening. Listening well and respecting the ability of others to comprehend, and to have the patience to accept or respond to what is heard, can lead to attunement with one another.

Attunement

The best gift we can give someone who shares a traumatic story is to be an active listener. Active listening and attunement, which go hand in hand, are powerful interventions a client experiences in the therapy room. Attunement, another way of naming empathy, is the capacity for the caring person to be fully present by tuning in to the feelings and experiences of the cared-for person. Active listening is a skill that takes practice because it is not how most of us engage in conversation. We most often see conversation as a dialogue, a give-and-take by both sides. Active listening is usually practiced in a caring relationship, and it is not a dialogue. The cared-for person does the majority of the talking, while the caring person concentrates on actively listening to them. Sounds simple, right? Believe it or not, most people have had little practice doing this and struggle to really listen. That's why we need to practice and develop the skill of active listening.

Active listening involves staying attuned to what the speaker is talking about and then reflecting back to them what you have heard. Active listening does not question the person's words, nor does it interrogate or give off even a whiff of investigation. Nor does an active listener provide feedback. Active listening does not interrupt the flow of the cared-for's thoughts. Here is an example of how it might look:

> **Speaker:** "I cannot believe the day I had at work today."
>
> **Listener:** "Today was a lot." (Notice this is a statement, not a question.)
>
> **Speaker:** "Yes. It started with my drive in. Two of the roads I took to work were closed because of construction. Which means I got to work late today and I was late for the 9:00 a.m. meeting I had scheduled with my team."
>
> **Listener:** "Two roads closed today, which made you late for your meeting."
>
> **Speaker:** "Exactly! I was so embarrassed at being late that I was flustered while in my meeting."
>
> **Listener:** "So you got to work embarrassed and then felt flustered in your meeting."
>
> **Speaker:** "I was *so* flustered. It took forever to recover and feel like myself."
>
> **Listener:** "It took awhile to feel like yourself after getting to work."

Active listening reveals to the speaker that they have the floor and they can take as much time as they need. When the caring person repeats what they have heard to the cared-for person, it also clarifies that listening occurred. When the caring person repeats something inaccurately, or if the cared-for person questions what the caring person says, the cared-for will speak up and say something. This doesn't mean the caring person was not listening. It just means the cared-for is thinking through what they said because the caring person reflected it back to them in a way the cared-for is not sure of. This is attunement, and it can be a very powerful antidote to trauma. Where trauma leaves us feeling isolated, alone, and unsupported, attunement whispers that we are seen and heard and valued. Attunement shows a person that someone is present and listening, spending valuable time with them. Attunement empowers a person to give voice to their emotions and experiences.

One of the classes I (Adrienne) was required to take in my counseling master's program was called Listening Skills. Every week we attended class, but most students dreaded it. Not because it was hard but because each week, two people were pulled to the front of the class to practice active listening while everyone else watched. For a whole semester, these conversations between two people practiced the skills we discussed. To me it all sounded like hogwash. I thought there was no way anyone was going to feel cared for and listened to after having a conversation like this.

So I practiced one night on my unknowing husband. He got home from work and my experiment started. He talked about his day and I listened actively. I repeated back to him what I heard him saying. I never interjected a question or my own thoughts or feelings. He spoke and shared and went a great deal into the day he'd had. When the experiment was over, it was time to check in with the cared-for. How did he feel about the conversation we'd just had? Did he notice anything? Did it feel different? His response: "I have never felt so listened to in my whole life." My experiment did not prove what I thought it would. It proved that what most of us are longing for when we talk is that we really would just like someone to be there to listen to us and let us be the focus for a few minutes. One of the biggest takeaways I had from that conversation was that active listening encourages the cared-for to keep sharing. The floor was his, and it opened the door for me to learn so much about him, and I saw how much he appreciated being heard.

Churches cannot practice listening to one another each Sunday. But churches can nurture small groups in which active listening can occur. In fact, good listening skills can be modeled in the group and become great examples of learning by example. When Kris and I (Scot) drive home from our small groups, we often go over what we heard from others. What occurs nearly every time is that one of us will have heard something the other did not. (Truth be told, Kris is the one who hears the most and I am the one who did not hear.) These pockets of small groups where people hear one another and are heard can be expanded when churches or institutions provide regular social gatherings where groups mix with one another.

Decision-Making

Trauma forms a sense that a person in the trauma zone lacks choice. A victim doesn't choose to be hurt, neglected, abused, abandoned, or steamrolled. Part of healing occurs when the survivor re-experiences choice and autonomy. Giving their choice back empowers a person to make their own decisions. The caring person needs to take a step back from taking the lead. The caring person honors the cared-for person. Honor helps the cared-for person to build their strength and skills so they can be in charge of their decisions. Empowerment encourages a victim to discover the strength they have inside. The caring person works for the cared-for to help them find that power. The caring person wants the cared-for not to think they have to rely on the caring person's confidence and power.

The wife of a pastor at a very large and busy church was pregnant with their first child. The couple's journey to pregnancy had been long and challenging, including multiple miscarriages and even surgery. But now this young couple was weeks away from the baby's due date. She went into labor and went to triage. The husband knew his pastoral work would be limited when the baby came. He felt the stress of trying to decide whether to leave work to be with her. The church had told him that he would not get a lot of time off. So he chose to remain at work, to wait to hear whether this was active labor or just another false alarm. Unfortunately, their beautiful baby boy passed away while mom was in active labor. She was alone in the hospital during the hardest moment of her life. Her rock and support was still at work waiting to be updated. The church had formed an insensitive policy, and the pastor himself had decided to "follow the rules." But that left his wife vulnerable in the trauma zone. It was an unwise policy and an insensitive decision.

The pastor and his wife eventually left that church because of the trauma. A few months later, the pastor was called to a different church, but they both were still in the trauma zone. They sought trauma counseling and worked to put their lives back together. They were very focused on taking care of themselves and healing. One thing the woman found herself doing is communicating very clearly to her husband and to the church what she needed in this time. Her husband listened well, and so did the church. She had found that her depression set in when she was home alone. Being alone triggered the conditions that set so much of the trauma in motion. Her body was not ready to handle things on her own; she needed support. She also found that she felt regulation when she was close to her husband. So she came to work with him, even sitting in on his worship rehearsals. The church stepped up and supported her being wherever she needed to be, whenever she needed to be there. The church allowed this couple to have a voice and to take care of each other.

Let's Take This to the Church Briefly

Trauma-informed principles are helpful in many organizational settings. They can be applied by bosses, directors, administrators, employees, volunteers, and those being ministered to. In a church or ministry, we should ask whether the organization is empowering its staff. If a church is working to become a safe place for its congregants, we should ask, Is the day-to-day work environment one that empowers and supports the staff? When leadership is trauma informed in working with its staff, the staff will be more likely to pass on these trauma-safe pillars to those around them. Empowerment involves elevating unheard voices. If you are attending a church that has a high staff turnover rate, there usually is a reason why people do not stay very long. Leadership that wants to share power and responsibility will typically involve staff in decision-making, provide access to policies and procedures, clarifying how those policies and procedures were made, and elicit feedback that encourages growth and change.[9] When leadership leads under these trauma-informed principles, they model how employees and staff should interact with people.

We often are afraid to hear stories of hurt and abuse. We tend to turn away from the trauma stories around us. When we do this, we limit and oftentimes silence the victims' voices. We turn our backs on a necessary part of victims' healing journey. Listening empowers someone else to be heard. Empowerment through listening gives a voice back to the wounded and unheard. Listening involves a unique set of skills. It also involves letting things be messy and chaotic for a time, if needed. Empowerment lifts up those around us. When churches are in the trauma zone, the skill of listening that empowers those who have not been heard is a step forward in the healing process. Listening like this, however, requires that we listen to all and not just to one person or one story.

Chapter 14

Cultural Awareness

Humility in its basic form is having an honest and realistic view of ourselves in the context of knowing others. Humility, then, is both a personal and a social virtue. Humility is understanding that we do not know everything we need to know. It is also being aware that other people are the experts on their own lives. Humility is understanding that we know (at least partially) ourselves and understand our upbringing and culture, but that we should not impose ourselves on everyone around us. Humility is about serving others from a true perception of ourselves. Humility requires honesty in our words and responses, and growth in our ability to see life as a series of invitations rather than inconveniences. Humility nurtures diversity and respects the cultures of the different people we come into contact with. Humility also means knowing that there will always be more to learn about ourselves, others, and life, and understanding that at times we will be wrong.

Cultural humility requires that we acknowledge that the only culture we are experts on is our own. And if we are truly humble, we should admit we aren't really experts at all! Once we admit (humbly) our lack of mastering even our own culture, we will learn to be humbler about cultures outside of our own.

I (Scot) have visited Ireland (the republic, Catholic, south) and Northern Ireland (Protestant), and my intuitions about either Ireland or Northern Ireland are woefully inadequate to speak intelligently enough to resonate with the Irish of either sort. I've also been to South Africa, and even though I have spent several weeks in that beautiful country, I need to hold my intuitions in check there as well. When I hear friends from other countries talk about the American political scene, my sense is that they don't understand us well enough for them to say at least some of what they say. I'm not defending America when I say Europeans don't understand us. What I'm saying is that it takes years of immersion in a culture to come to terms with the instincts of that culture. (Admission: When I see that someone has traveled to a foreign country and wants to write an essay or a book about that culture, I click to another webpage.)

What is true about foreign countries is true about our siblings in our common (but not identical) faith. Each person grows up in a singular family and a community with its own schools of education. Each person finds a career on their own path, and when we meet one another, we bring our own cultures with us. Our cultures are as silent as the shelves that hold our books, but they are what support us.

Trauma-informed and trauma-safe cultures at any kind of Christian organization require the leaders of those cultures to understand that most of the time, we are in the presence of people in the trauma zone, and especially so on Sundays. Cultural humility about where others are reveals to us that we need to be better listeners. We all need to learn how trauma works in individuals, societies, and especially Christian organizations. Typically, most leaders are trauma uninformed and far too many are also resistant to becoming trauma sensitive. The church is a small sample of our society, which itself is growing in its trauma sensitivities, but the church (as it usually is on social issues) is behind society in this area. When American culture was publishing #MeToo stories, the church remained silent until a bold woman stepped forward with a #ChurchToo hashtag, setting off a storm of storytelling. Truth be told, some Christian organizations listened well, some barely listened and hoped it would all go away, and some flat out resisted the stories as hysteria and false narratives.[1] Building connected relationships within a safe environment forms the roots of all our trauma-safe principles. Trauma-informed leadership strives to prevent retraumatization while building safe and secure connections for growth and healing. This final pillar of culture building contends that Christian organizations and ministries should replicate, and perhaps improve on, American society's great gains over the last few decades. So in essence, this final pillar invites us to define our identity. It asks us to ponder where we are on a social map and to take this step with humility, knowing we have something to learn about ourselves and others. This is why we call the sixth pillar "cultural awareness."

In 2001 Pamela Hays developed the ADDRESSING model to help us process where we are in a socially-informed multidimensional concept of our identity. This model presents ten elements to consider:[2]

1. Age and generational influences
2. Developmental or other disabilities
3. Disabilities acquired later in life
4. Religion and spiritual orientation
5. Ethnic and racial identity
6. Socioeconomic status
7. Sexual orientation
8. Indigenous heritage
9. National origin
10. Gender

Each of these elements influences our identity, how we see ourselves, and how the world around us sees us. Most of us perceive these elements only at the instinctual level rather than at the conscious and informed level. But each identity marker influences the friends we make, our family culture, the trauma we may have experienced, and how we are treated by others. Our identity, formed from these markers, creates societal norms and stereotypes and expectations and evaluations and judgments. Our cultural identity plays a significant role in being trauma informed because it is something all people bring to the table. We all have a culture, a background, a story. Some of these identity markers may lead to cultural comments or actions that other us and discriminate against us.

Leaders of organizations need to keep in mind that when someone admits they have experienced trauma or are in the trauma zone (which falls under the first *D* in the list, developmental or other disabilities) they may experience prejudice or discrimination. Cultural humility gives us the skill to recognize where others are. They may mention they are seeing a mental health therapist only to get a response, spoken or not, that reflects a lack of cultural humility, communicating, "What's wrong? Can't you handle it!" People seeking to heal from trauma may be hurt or retraumatized by the very thing that makes them unique. This is why, in a broader sense, it is important that we understand our own identity markers. When we understand what marks us as distinct from others, we become more equipped to look at what makes others unique. By seeing and acknowledging our different identities, we grow in awareness that we are bringing something unique to the table in a relationship. Slowing down and acknowledging the differences in everyone around us also opens us up to the idea that everyone around us can teach us something about them. Humility steps in and we adopt the role of student.

Differences can make being in community together healthy or harmful. Saying something insensitive, racist, or judgmental is harmful. Discrimination because of cultural, historical, or identity-based factors has a detrimental impact on opportunities and advancement as well as mental health. Broad evaluative comments about others often create an us-versus-them environment in which there is an ingroup and an outgroup, and we typically put ourselves in the ingroup. We may do this because we feel anxious or threatened. We all want safety and connection. We want to belong. But we may seek that in harmful ways. Us-versus-them cultures are toxic and do not align with authentic biblical community.

Here are a few insights from the Scriptures that inform the kind of healthy community we are seeking to develop and nurture as a trauma-safe space:

1. We are all made in God's image (Gen. 1:27).
2. God desires covenant with all humans (Genesis 12).
3. The prophets looked for a day when the nations would pour into Israel (Isaiah 40–66).
4. Jesus reached out to those on the margins, the poor, the abused, and the wounded (Matt. 9:36).
5. In Christ we are all one (Gal. 3:28), with gentiles being gentiles and Jews being Jews (Romans 13–15).
6. The kingdom of God will be made up of people from around the globe, and the numbers will never get to the end of the names and people (Rev. 5:9–10).

Because number 6 is so important, I want to cite the verses that support it (italics added):

> And they sang a new song, saying:
>
> "You are worthy to take the scroll
> and to open its seals,

> because you were slain,
> and with your blood you purchased for God
> *persons from every tribe and language and people and nation.*
> You have made them to be a kingdom and priests to serve our God,
> and they will reign on the earth." (NIV)

Those terms are something akin to a first-century version of affirmative action, DEI, and multiculturalism: the gathering of people from all tribes and languages and peoples and nations. Those mentioned here are not being asked to give up the markers of their identity. Rather, John's Revelation affirms such diversity throughout eternity. Cultural humility affirms other cultures. A lack of cultural humility thinks these verses describe other cultures becoming what our own culture is. Example: A person without cultural humility thinks we will all sing praises to God in the kingdom in English. Cultural humility looks forward to the kingdom where each person will, as on the day of Pentecost in Acts 2, sing praises in their own language.

Developing a healthy culture for connection with others begins when we acknowledge the racial, gender, and class differences around us and then work to encourage and uplift those voices. If our staff and volunteers do not represent the community around us, how will our community feel invited, included, and welcomed? This effort must go beyond planting a Black man or woman on the platform of a majority white church so the audience can see some diversity. It goes beyond putting a woman on a committee to give the impression of inclusion. Even those who intentionally form multicultural churches are often accused of filling the seats of power with white men.[3] So what can be done to insure we are more effective?

Again, it starts by listening to the community, knowing people from other cultures, asking their advice, sharing power with those of other cultures, and surrendering our power to empower others in a culture of safety, mutuality, and trustworthiness. Don't count on change happening immediately. To change a culture takes a minimum of seven years of effort. The challenges of cultural diversity? Double it. But don't give up.[4] Keep listening. Keep adjusting.

In addition, demonstrate cultural awareness of your community. Many ministries and churches naturally want to reach out to the communities that surround them. But when people from those communities show up and discover, even intuitively, that they are not represented in leadership, the leadership is communicating that people have to look or present in a certain way to have a voice in this community.[5] If there is no diversity among the leadership, there is bias. As I (Scot) like to say, your leadership should not be all white unless you live in an all-white Swedish community in Nebraska. Understand that we are not claiming this bias is intentional or meant to be exclusive, but such systemic—even unintentional—exclusion is perceived as bias and prejudice. Those in the dominant culture—whatever it may be—need to be aware that they are communicating such bias and, as this pillar emphasizes, work to overcome it.

Diversity brings benefits and challenges. How can a homogenous team challenge their framework, opinions, and thoughts? Biases they are unaware they have will continue unchecked. Diversity brings outside thoughts and opinions and challenges us to understand, listen to, and grow from the insights and experiences of others. A lack of diversity can lead to marginalization of others, and marginalization can lead to trauma.

An adage I (Adrienne) have heard, though I don't know where it comes from, says, "What you win them with is what you win them to." Toward the end of COVID, many churches used their stance on the masking issue as a way to win people to come back to church or to change to their church. But if you use a political issue like masking to attract people, you risk that issue defining your community in ways you might not want or expect. The danger is that the cultural battles will inevitably change and the issue that brought people to your church may be at odds with the gospel of Jesus. Though you preach taking up your cross or loving the least of these, you may find people are more committed to their cultural or political battles.

If we win people to our churches or ministries by trying to make them representative of a particular issue or demographic—tailoring our message to attract one tribe over another—we are no longer representing the diverse beauty of the gospel inviting us to enter the kingdom of God. And yet there is another sense in which this approach can be helpful. For if our goal is to cultivate biblically informed, trauma-safe spaces that welcome those who have been hurt and traumatized, the best way to win them to our community is by modeling that kind of community.

Adding cultural awareness and humility to our repertoire for being trauma informed means we respect diversity and appreciate differences. Humility is also knowing that the story is not about us and that at times we will be culturally insensitive. We may say or do the wrong thing. The last pillar is awareness because it implies we are limited.

Cultural humility admits making mistakes and apologizes. I have experienced this quite a few times as a counselor. I have had clients come in to my office to speak about something I did or said in a previous session. They share how they experienced what I said. Cultural humility requires me to sit and listen, to understand what they heard and felt. Humility allows me to apologize for what I said or did, and that humility encourages their bravery for expressing themselves. What was said or done may not have been intentional, but saying sorry means you understand that it hurt.

Humility is a defining moment relationally. We have this modeled perfectly for us in the person of Jesus. Time and again we see him model humility. Philippians 2 shows us that he humbled himself. In this context, the apostle Paul appeals to the Philippians to be humble with one another by valuing others above themselves. This congregation was experiencing internal tensions (4:2–3) and external opposition (1:28). Evidently their unity was evaporating, and in that context Paul pulls out one of his favorite themes: Christians are to be like Christ. His key word is "humility" (2:3) and his example was Jesus himself. Jesus surrendered the glories of the Father's presence and entered time and space. But he did not just enter our world, he went to the ugliest feature of life on earth: the public desecration of a human being by crucifixion (2:6–8). Paul then reveals that beyond that kind of others-serving life lies the glory of a return to the presence of God (2:9–11). In our terms, Paul exhorts Christians to let the cruciform life of Jesus shape our relations with others. How? Humility. We work at cultural humility because we have chosen to follow Christ.

This makes me think of so many of the raw and honest stories that people have entrusted to us that show up in this book. These people needed to be listened to. Each of them encountered individuals who didn't understand the humility needed to sit with the wounded. Many of these people needed someone to be willing to say they were sorry for not getting it right the first time. Humility embraces the trauma of others as an opportunity. Their trauma becomes an invitation to serve others and so empower them toward healing, not to swoop in, do damage control, and save the day. If we want to be a trauma-informed church or ministry, we will serve with trauma-informed principles that nurture a trauma-safe environment for all.

In our concluding chapter, we'll share a story of a trauma-growing church and give you a few ideas for how to become more trauma sensitive, while also keeping our eye on the story of Paul and the Corinthian church.

PART 4

Trauma Healthy

THE WHOLE BODY

Chapter 15

Striving for Trauma-Healthy Spaces

A church we know had gone through a difficult time with a pastor and his assistant. Both had been "let go," which is the language we often use for "got fired." True to many church situations, the church's story was not told as transparently as it could have been. The result was about what you might expect.

Some in the church were convinced that letting the pastor and his assistant go was the right thing to do. Others in the church were convinced that both were mistreated. This second group was not happy, and the first group was not happy with the second group. The groups were at odds with one another and the tension was palpable. People took sides. Where people sat on Sunday morning, which Sunday school class they attended, and which small group they participated in—every decision reflected the side they had taken. The tension bubbled over into anger, resentment, and dissatisfaction with everything the leaders were deciding. Labels were tossed at one another, and assumptions flew around the community without any attempt to talk with those about whom the assumptions were being made.

Gossip could have destroyed this church. Strategies for "winning the war" were formed. People on both sides were in the trauma zone, with several on both sides traumatizing those on the other side. Of course, some stayed out of the fray entirely. Some people left. What was clear to the leaders was that people no longer trusted one another.

What we have just described happens from time to time in almost every church. The details and specifics vary, but most churches that have survived at least a generation or two typically experience a conflict or disagreement that leads to division. Tensions between groups taking opposite sides is as old as Jerusalem's first church (Acts 6), and it was more than true about Paul's house churches in Corinth. But how should we handle church tensions where people are commonly wounded and abused and end up in the trauma zone? Before we can look at how this typical and traumatic church split progressed toward a trauma-healthy church, let's return to the apostle Paul and review a strategy he used to deal with disagreement and division.

Paul Again

We began this book with an introductory look at the basics of trauma: the four responses of fight, flight, freeze, and fawn. We then looked at the apostle Paul and his interactions with the church at Corinth and saw how he dealt with the trauma he experienced in his relationship with that church. Paul was not afraid of conflict, but as we saw earlier, his letters show that he chose to flee the situation in Corinth so he could find safety in places like Ephesus and Macedonia. We don't know for sure, but this may have been to give himself time to produce a fight response against unjust allegations. Fighting back was his *modus operandi* whenever Paul was accused.

We've been seeking to learn from Paul, though we are not arguing that we ought to follow Paul in every way. Paul was not perfect. Jesus is the only perfect one. And so Paul's way of fighting back does not grant us a biblical warrant to get ugly ourselves when we fight back. Still, his experience of trauma does speak across the millennia to inform us today. And as we continue to look at Paul, we see that fighting was not Paul's only response to trauma. In this final chapter, I (Scot) hope to explore the most fascinating and gospel-shaped response of Paul as he explored his own trauma zone. I hesitate to call it his "winning strategy," but there are worse ways to describe what Paul was doing.

I believe Paul fawned. Yes, the mighty, lionlike apostle fawned. But his fawning was not the typical capitulation to critics, nor did he accept his abuse to avoid further criticism. Paul did not duck to stay out of the fray. I say this because our standard understanding of fawning is that one surrenders to their abuser and capitulates: gives in, gives up, endures the pain and abuse, taking it on the chin, and refrains from fighting back or fleeing. As we saw in earlier chapters, psychologists call fawning hypoarousal. A fawning person gives up any chance of fighting or fleeing and instead seeks to have the abuser like them by making themselves more appealing.

Paul does this in an almost mocking, sarcastic, and ironic manner. He fawns before the Corinthians by adapting to his critics' expectations. What distinguishes Paul's manner of fawning is that it was also a way of fighting back in an altogether fresh and Christian manner. Paul fawned not by surrendering to the opinions and demands of his critics but by following the rubric of a radically different theology of life and leadership. We call his approach "gospel fawning." Paul's gospel fawning subverted the powers that abused and wounded him. To use a phrase well studied by Michael Gorman, Paul's gospel fawning was an experiment in cruciform leadership,[1] or to use another term, Christoform living.[2] What I'm referring to as Paul's fawning was not a hypoarousal mask hiding a hyperarousal fight. Instead, Paul developed a form of life that took refuge, formed his self-identity, and found safety in identifying with the suffering of Jesus himself. He reshaped the negatives (criticism and suffering) into a radical positive (sharing the way of Jesus).

Paul's gospel fawning was something of a paradox. Paul subversively fawned for his critics by searching for and finding safety and security in the pattern of Jesus' death. He trusted Christ not only for salvation but for a pattern of survival. From this position of Spirit-born safety, he could flee, fight back, and resist the ways his opponents in Corinth were treating him. Paul turned his trauma into a means of Christlike living and his traumatic suffering into an opportunity to suffer with Christ. His trauma became a means of demonstrating the cross life, not because he wanted to suffer but to show how the gospel could reshape his trauma, not by pretending but by immersing his inner world in Jesus' life.

I believe there is potential for a profoundly gospel-shaped experience for us today in the trauma zone. Gospel-shaped fawning is not a trick of the mind or an appeal to positive thinking. Rather, gospel-shaped fawning is a way of appropriating the resistance and revolution of the crucifixion that led to resurrection and glorification, just as Paul explains in Philippians 2.

From a clinical standpoint, gospel fawning is both subversive and a means of fighting back. Since all trauma responses are about survival, gospel fawning is a means of battling for safety. Some who are in the trauma zone fight power structures because they believe their best way to resolve the problem is to directly confront it. By contrast, fawning in its standard sense searches for acceptance from others and chooses not to fight back, at least not in the way the world fights back. Fawning is about making yourself small to let someone else be big. Typical fawning clearly lacks healthy boundaries, but gospel fawners undermine typical fawning responses by asserting themselves with strength. They set their own boundaries based on the knowledge that they are accepted and loved because of who the Father has made them to be. Gospel fawning subverts the typical fawning response and attempts to win people over by loving them without letting them make you feel small and insignificant. It involves the sacrifice of letting someone else be big when they believe that is what they need, and it is a free choice a person makes, not something they are forced to do. Gospel fawners know themselves as loved by God, and they learn to know Christ more deeply by embracing his suffering as their suffering.

Gospel fawning—and this is key—entails the full human agency and personal choice of the one who has been abused. To be clear, this is not capitulation, nor does it communicate that the abuse of power can be redemptive. Gospel fawning does not legitimate emotional, physical, or professional violence but instead attempts to subvert violence in the name of the cross. I'll repeat this again so that it is clear: Gospel fawning is not something a person is coerced or manipulated into like typical fawning. Gospel fawning is rather a choice to communicate that even though a person is in the trauma zone, they are choosing to look to Christ for identity, security, and safety. Gospel fawning disarms those in power with the weapons of emotional warfare. Instead of drawing a sword, the gospel fawner pulls out a petition for peace. This approach copes with trauma theologically and is an affirmation of oneself in the knowledge that God has affirmed Christ and those who belong to Christ. Paul, as it were, baptized his own trauma in the cross and suffering of Christ, not to legitimate his suffering at the hands of those abusing him but to subvert it with a message of victory through and over his suffering.

It's All About Character

Running like a trickling stream throughout our book is something we've hinted at, but not fully discussed. It's that what matters most in forming a trauma-healthy environment in a Christian organization is character. Jesus taught this truth using a helpful image: "Thus, every good tree makes beautiful fruit, but a diseased tree makes evil fruit. A good tree isn't able to make evil fruit, nor is a diseased tree [able] to make beautiful fruit" (Matt. 7:17–18). For an organization to nurture a trauma-healthy culture, the people leading the process need to be people of character. We mention this here because the gospel fawning we are talking about was more than a technique, it was an expression of Paul's character, a character deeply shaped by the gospel of Jesus Christ.

Character expresses a person's moral personhood, which in turn expresses a pattern of goodness in choices and practices. Good persons are trauma informed and, because of their character, are instinctually trauma sensitive. Because they are a person of a certain character, they nurture a trauma-safe and eventually trauma-healthy environment. Trauma sensitivity is the "beautiful fruit" that grows on a "good tree." The trauma-uninformed and the trauma-insensitive person cannot yield a trauma-healthy space, whether in a church or a Christian organization.

Character, then, is the tree that bears the fruit as a person is formed. In a book I wrote on character, I (Scot) borrowed a definition from authors Michael Cox and Brad Kallenberg to inform my own definition of Christian character:

> "Character denotes the particular set of qualities, both natural and acquired, that serves to identify a person or community." The authors Cox and Kallenberg continue in ways echoing what was just written: "in the context of Christian ethics, character names an established disposition (or set of dispositions) with respect to the particular conception of the good exemplified by Christ. Such character is developed over time and, as such, can be formed either toward or away from virtues, understood as those intellectual

> and affective habits that enable the pursuit of excellence [=*tov*]." Christian integrity measures a person acting consistently with one's character as measured by Jesus' own life. Character, therefore, is, in outline form:
>
> One's basic personality
> shaped or unshaped over time by virtue or vice
> resulting in consistent moral traits in that person.
>
> The question we need to ask is if our churches shape character or do they value performance? The answer fuzzes and fizzes between the two but our conversations with pastor after congregant in the last three years convinces us that a church retooled to form character is more of a revolution than a reformation, and it will require more than change and shift. It will require transformation.[3]

Forming trauma-healthy churches is at the root of grace-shaped and Spirit-formed transformation of character. Trauma-healthy churches and Christian ministries are the fruit of good character, and people of character are what we need to lead churches out of social trauma zones into spaces of reconciliation and peace.

The Traumatized Are the Best Witnesses of God's Grace

Persons in a trauma zone will seek safety, and one way they do this is by retreating into their inner lives. They will often affirm key truths such as:

- I am loved by God.

- My identity is in Christ (not in what my critic is saying).
- I take solace in that I did my best.
- God is with me.
- That person just doesn't like me.
- Others recognize my giftedness.

By retreating, that person has entered into an inner fawning that shields them from outward criticism and attack. We consider this a healthy form of fawning, a necessary step in what we are calling gospel fawning. While some would reserve the term *fawning* solely to designate an unhealthy capitulation to the powers at work against a traumatized person, in explaining Paul we need to grapple with how he turned his suffering into hope. My proposal is that he subverted his trauma by identifying his suffering with Jesus' rejection and suffering. In this, he identified with Jesus in such a way that he experienced the cross of Christ and then entered the tomb with Jesus to experience resurrection. Gospel fawning, as practiced by Paul, is what we practice as well to experience the victory of a resurrection life.

We know that when ministering in Corinth, the apostle and his associates chose to refuse funding from the Corinthians. To acquire money for their needs, Paul and his coworkers did manual labor instead. As we mentioned earlier, by doing this Paul degraded his status—over and over—to degrade the triumphalism and status mongering of the Corinthians. To put it another way, Paul fell down (fawned) and let the Corinthians win their status game, choosing an alternate path of self-denial, which became his embodied witness to the Corinthians of the way of Christ. While this appeared to be unmanly to the Corinthians, it was a subversive act indicating that Paul was playing by a different set of rules and values.

Here are some of Paul's own words, words that surely got under the skin and reddened the faces of his Corinthian hobnobbers. Here I have chosen to use my own translation because it evokes the graphic language Paul flashed before them. Paul classifies himself with the "idiots" of their world. As you read what Paul wrote, imagine someone in Paul's own circle reading Paul's letters to the Corinthians with Paul absent, and then imagine what the status-minded people of Corinth must have been thinking of Paul's vision of Christ crucified:

> Because "God's idiocy" is wiser than humans' and "God's weakness" is stronger than humans'. For look at your calling, siblings, that not many are wise consistent with flesh, not many powerful, not many noble. But God selected the Kosmos's idiots to degrade the wise, and God elected the Kosmos's weak to degrade the strong, and God elected the Kosmos's ignoble and devalued—the ones who "are not"—to undo the ones who "are," so that no flesh may boast before God. (1 Cor. 1:25–29 *Second Testament*)

Another example, again in my own translation:

> For it looks like God has demonstrated us—the Commissioners—last, as death-bound, that we have become theater to the Kosmos and to envoys and humans.
>
> [Sarcastic again]
>
> We are "idiots" because of Christos. You are "prudent" in Christos.
>
> We are "weak." You are "strong."
>
> You are in "splendor." We are "dishonored."
>
> Up to the present hour we hunger and we thirst and are shabby and slapped and destabilized and we labor, working with our own hands.
>
> In snubbing, we bless;
> in being chased, we put up [with it];

in dissing, we console.

We have become like the Kosmos's trash, the compost of all—until the present. (1 Cor. 4:9–13)

Let's face it: Knowing people to be what they are, Paul's ideas probably saw no more success in Corinth than such efforts would today. What Paul said was antithetical to the values of this world, the Kosmos. I was once speaking with a theologian about his nationwide ministry among Roman Catholics when, in the middle of our conversation, he suddenly burst out, and I quote him verbatim, "I'm nothing but a piece of horse dung." *Well*, I thought to myself, *I think your ideas are breathtakingly fresh and important, and I think you are gifted by God, and I surely don't think of you as a big pile of dung on the street after a parade.* This man was clearly expressing humility and the power of God's grace in his life by imitating the apostle Paul. And I certainly wasn't willing to go to the extreme of thinking of him as publicly discarded defecation. That's likely how Paul's status-conscious opponents in Corinth were thinking: "Paul, you are taking all of this a bit too far." Paul, however, is doing this intentionally to subvert their sense of status in his response, flipping the entire script so that what they think highly of, that of supposed high status, was brought low, and what was of low status was raised high. Only by living out one's low status, Paul contended, does one become a useful and significant instrument of God's gracious power.

Let's consider one final example, and it must be read slowly with echoes of Paul's disability status in mind. It shows us again how Paul confronts and subverts the status-mongering group that was opposing him in Corinth:

> Therefore, in order to keep me from becoming conceited, I was given a thorn in my flesh, a messenger of Satan, to torment me. Three times I pleaded with the Lord to take it away from me. But

> he said to me, "My grace is sufficient for you, for my power is made perfect in weakness." Therefore I will boast all the more gladly about my weaknesses, so that Christ's power may rest on me. That is why, for Christ's sake, I delight in weaknesses, in insults, in hardships, in persecutions, in difficulties. For when I am weak, then I am strong. (2 Cor. 12:7–10 NIV)

Here we see it all: a mix of sarcasm and fawning all wrapped up with some indirect self-defensiveness—it becomes the man! He's giving in by not giving in. He's losing their status game but winning in his inner world and the kingdom of God by pointing to his status enhancement in Christ. His weakness, he contends, promotes God's strength. His disability reveals his divine ability. Paul was not released from his thorn in the flesh; rather that thorn revealed God's power at work in and through him. Here Paul's gospel fawning is used to subvert the very powers that made fawning the typical and expected way for people to cow to their authority.

Admittedly, Paul's weapons seem weird. He is choosing to resist by giving in, letting them score a win for their status-mongering way of life while simultaneously showing them how he chooses to walk a different and better path by following the one crucified. As Philip Plyming, who has himself suffered deep abuses, recently wrote about Paul's suffering,

> Informed by the value system of secular Corinth, according to whose way they seem to be walking, the Corinthian believers apparently expected to see God at work in places of physical strength, material success, social achievement, human flourishing, lasting smiles and rhetorical brilliance. [But] Paul's stories of his own suffering challenge these assumptions head-on. He tells stories of God both present and at work in very different places, places of his own hardship that were patterned on the cross of Christ and suffused with

> God's resurrection power. In those experiences which invited such shame and ridicule within ancient Corinth—physical weakness, emotional brokenness and social humiliation—Paul proudly witnesses to God at work in enduring and hopeful ways. . . . [T]he Corinthians thought they knew where they could see God at work. Paul's stories challenged them to look somewhere altogether different and see God at work in some surprising places—in their own Good Fridays.[4]

Where the typical Roman world would have seen Paul fawning or flopping, Paul flipped the very values they were boasting and glorying in—though boasting not in the victory they sought but in his loss, boasting in the crucifixion as the means to resurrection.

Those who are in the trauma zone are seeking safety. Paul finds his safety in fighting back, in fleeing, and then in fawning in a most unusual way. In each of these ways, Paul not only illustrates and confirms the reality of his trauma, giving us indicators to recognize trauma in our own lives, but he provides us with a map to begin healing from trauma. As we finish our study of Paul, we want to appropriate what we have learned and to consider what we today can do to begin healing and finding a trauma-healthy space in life. When those in the trauma zone choose to live by witnessing to God's grace and the strength it gives them, they reveal the very same thing Paul learned: In our weaknesses, God empowers us.

Enjoy Your Hobbies

So let's get practical by looking at what happens when churches face division. How do they deal with the resulting trauma and tension? The first step is to remember that you aren't doing this alone. Facing trauma requires a support team, so you need to find others around you who can bring you strength and encouragement. This need will be evident as we complete the story we began earlier. Along with finding others for support, it is also important to return to things you love doing or even find some new activities to enjoy. It might be photography or creating art, or walking through the woods and looking for birds, or reading your favorite novelist. Whatever your hobbies are, find ways to heal and gain strength by living in a relaxed body, because this is good for your well-being. Relaxed muscles signal to your brain that you are safe. And doing hobbies and activities that bring smiles, peace, and stability gives you a felt sense of safety. Hobbies can help you get back into your body and feel okay being there. As you enjoy doing something, you invest in being back in control of yourself.

It takes a village, so you may need to work at creating your own village for support and healing. Your village can include your therapist, your sage, a support group, and your friends. It will take time to create, but villages are adaptable and creative. What we have in mind, however, is simply finding other people who can help you in the trauma zone and aid in your healing. This village, then, is your trauma-healthy space. And our prayer in writing this book is that more and more churches will become those trauma-healthy spaces.

Get a Therapist

Many people who have experienced trauma cannot simply jump right back into complicated relationships and communities. Intricate and complex work needs to be done to heal from trauma, especially in a way that does not create even more trauma. When this is not done correctly, reliving your trauma can create more trauma and lead to more triggers. Because of this, we advise seeking professionals who are trained in trauma therapy who can provide insight as well as the relief and support that are needed to do this difficult work. You may find yourself in a place where, like I (Adrienne) was, you are questioning your experiences and your story. You may need support and trust before you can even begin to understand your trauma. Therapists are often able to help you slowly unpack the trauma, but there is no one right way to do this. Evidence shows that all trauma modalities, when done to efficacy, are roughly 80 percent effective. A few options you might consider are eye movement desensitization and reprocessing (EMDR), cognitive processing therapy (CPT), and exposure and response prevention (ERP). It's best to ask your therapist what they recommend.

A therapist may even suggest you try doing what Paul did, though they may not know this was Paul's response. They may suggest that you subvert your trauma with some hard-nosed gospel fawning. Your therapist will help you come to terms with your anger and find healthy ways to express it, and over time you may find yourself identifying closely with Paul's sarcasm, self-defenses, over-the-top language, labeling, and various emotions, especially those expressed in 2 Corinthians 10–13.

Find at Least One Sage

While finding a trauma therapist is a great first step in building support, finding a wise individual who checks in with you regularly also helps. You can lean into a sage in your life, and this person can help you build a more supportive base. In the example of the church at the close of this chapter, we will see the value of having wise leaders. A therapist is one element of support, but their support primarily takes place within the therapy office during a clear time limit. If you visit them once a week, you will get one hour of support for that week, but every week has another 168 hours. Don't worry! It is natural and human to need more than one hour a week of support.

This additional support can also come from a mentoring relationship that involves extended conversations with open-ended time limits. With a sage or mentor, you give that person permission to know what is going on inside your life. A sage is different from a friend in that the relationship is focused on the sage guiding you on a path they may have already walked. This person is often a few steps ahead of you in their own journey, and they can provide insight into places and situations they have already been, places you may just be exploring. They offer a different and hopefully wiser perspective. And they care about your journey and your growth.

Support Groups

Additionally, you can find help when you are in the trauma zone by developing a support group. Support groups offer a unique perspective where you have the opportunity to walk alongside people who can also say "I've been there." They truly get you. This support can be a balm to the hurt you have experienced when you feel no one understands you. You may feel alone and misunderstood. Support groups put words to what you are feeling or to an experience that a trauma survivor has no words for.

Friends

A therapist is helpful, as is a sage or mentor, and there is great value in a support group, but the most common form of support in daily life is from a friend. A good, understanding friend can help you in the middle of the day when you are struggling at work. You can reach out to them and have someone to talk to when you are home at night. They can get you out of the house, distract you from things you need to not think about or even stay away from. They provide the support you need day to day, the kind of support that a therapist cannot provide.

Before We Finish Our Story

Before we conclude, let's review where we've been.

First, remember what trauma is. While there are times when a person will self-diagnose, more often we need others to diagnose a condition of trauma. The traumatized person experiences anxiety, depression, and heightened awareness of the senses, feeling like they need to be totally alert. They can be angry, scared, stunned, untrusting, agitated, and confused. If any of these symptoms are present in your life, therapy might be the best first step forward.

Second, we've pointed out that congregations need to recognize the power they wield and to recognize their abuse of other congregants as well as their leaders. Congregations have power—just ask Paul! And this is especially true of congregations with a more congregational polity—when a church's power rests mostly in the people, who are able to vote leaders in or out. In such churches, the congregation has power and authority over the leadership. Congregations in other polities—presbyterian or episcopal, for example—may not have the power of voting, but they can vote with the absence of butts in the seats or bills in the plate. Sometimes they wield power through manipulatively meeting with the leaders or by protesting in other ways. At times congregations or a group in the church can become abusive in their capacity to vote, protest, or use their voice. They may write emails to one another or to a group of people.

Third, we hope you have begun to see why churches need to become trauma informed. This isn't just the latest trend to jump on. It's a diagnosis that has the potential to bring healing to hurting people. I (Adrienne) can't reinvent the wheel designed by the Substance Abuse and Mental Health Services Administration (SAMHSA). That wheel has six spokes, or principles, that mark trauma-informed practices in an institution, which we have adapted in this book for trauma-informed congregations and Christian institutions.[5] SAMHSA has a valuable wide-reaching definition of trauma: "Trauma results from an event, series of events, or set of circumstances that is experienced by an individual as physically or emotionally harmful or threatening and that has lasting adverse effects on the individual's functioning and physical, social, emotional, or spiritual well-being."

And how do these principles shape trauma-informed practices? A program, organization, or system that is trauma informed:

- *Realizes* the widespread impact of trauma and understands potential paths for recovery.
- *Recognizes* signs and symptoms in clients, families, staff, and others involved with systems.
- *Responds* by fully integrating knowledge about trauma into policies, procedures, and practices.
- Seeks to *resist retraumatization*.[6]

As we conclude, we hope to illustrate how these six principles can be lived out with a real-world example, looking at how a church that was divided and split was able to turn around and experience healing, eventually becoming a trauma-safe community.

A Story Now Completed

The first step toward reconciliation in any conflict resolution is the restoration of trust. Teresa Morgan, in her new study *Trust in Atonement*, summarizes recent studies on the importance of trust as reconciliation begins to form between embattled persons or groups. Building trust across the aisle requires accepting that those on the "other side" are decent, competent humans, and that they are compassionate enough to ponder trusting them. What sits rather silently and often invisibly in this first step is risk, the willingness to take that first step.[7]

A wise pastor on the staff of our divided church, after spending lots of time listening to the disaffected, took that first step. He decided the best way forward was to listen to both the words and the hearts of those who were convinced the release of the pastor and his assistant were wrong. They gathered with a couple of wise leaders and prepared everyone for a conversation with prayers and short readings followed by some words of comfort, assuring each person of safety. People were encouraged to talk if they wanted to, and the leaders provided a safe space within that safe space by acknowledging that some might want to talk to a smaller group of only one or two others. Some of the people split into small groups to share wounds and disappointments. The morning bled into early afternoon until people began packing up their purses and hats and coats. Tears were dried and people hugged as a sign they were still linked to one another. People felt heard, even though they knew that those who had been released would not be returning. People of character and grace rose to the surface to lead.

However, this listening group was one-sided—it was held for only one side of the church. And some on the other side of the issue were justifiably suspicious. We mention this because without character and grace and trust, sessions like these can do plenty of damage as well as good. Some things may be said that are better left unsaid. Some attitudes can end up being hardened while some attitudes can be softened. Listening sessions do not always reach the ultimate goal of healing trauma, but they are an important step because the wounded need to know their voices are heard. I (Scot) would guess that Paul had some small group chats of his own with his close associates, and I would presume that some of the Corinthians were meeting in small groups to offer their complaints about Paul. Both sides deserved a hearing, and the same is true today. Churches will never be a safe place if only one side of a story is heard.

What followed that listening session? Some wanted to do it again because it felt so good to be heard. But their wise leaders discerned that another listening session was not the best next step. Instead, they advised the wounded to meet with therapists or with friends in the church and outside the church. The sermons also became more trauma sensitive, and those who had been traumatized began to feel safer. Some of those who were wounded chose to meet regularly with the pastor, even though the pastor knew he was not a therapist or trained in trauma therapy. But he did what he could. As a whole, the people walked onward, limping at times, hugging one another each Sunday morning or over coffee or meals. Some left the church because it was too painful. Their perception of that church, and at times of church itself, had been shattered. At times it was clear to them that safety meant safety only for some, safety only for those who agreed with the safety group.

Here is why this situation illustrates the principles and approach we've written about in this book. Those who were in the listening session discovered over and over that they could trust one another and that they were safe with one another. Individuals who were in the trauma zone began to trust themselves again. And when trust has formed, it can grow into trust expanded. A trauma-safe culture began to form, but this trauma-safe space was still composed only of those who had been in the listening session. Not surprisingly, some in the pro-release group were now doing the same: meeting together and forming safe spaces where trusting one another was palpable. Remember, this is a church, and churches are fellowships, so people of character and grace in both groups began to ponder and pray about meeting together to listen to one another. Was it possible or desirable for them to begin trusting those on the other side? Some took that risk, a risk that imitates what we've called Paul's gospel fawning. This effort of entering into other people's trauma zone with one's own trauma is risky and requires great vulnerability.

Mediators can help in this process, but mediators are not to be chosen *for* the groups in conflict. Mediators should be chosen and agreed upon *by* the groups in conflict. Names must emerge from the grassroots level. A mediator's essential skill is listening well enough to empathize with both sides. But for mediators to mediate, the various people involved need to trust the mediator, which is why mediators should not be chosen by the leaders. Two trustworthy leaders themselves became mediators, sometimes present in the meetings and sometimes not. An individual or two in the "safe culture" began to meet at times with individuals who thought the releases were not only right but necessary. These meetings were perceived not to be as safe as the listening session. Trusting was risky in this environment. As Teresa Morgan expresses it, "Sometimes taking an attitude of trust enables one to act with trust, and sometimes taking a step of trust enables the attitude to follow."[8] But still they decided to give it a try. They knew trusting was the only way to build a widespread safe culture. Soon some new relationships of trust formed and became the basis for an expanded culture of trust.

Though they did not use this term, these meetings were a practical exercise in what we have been calling gospel fawning. People on both sides embraced their own suffering by turning to Christ's sufferings. They learned for themselves Paul's rather abstract theology: that

Jesus found God to be trustworthy and so Jesus trusted God in his own suffering. They also learned that Jesus' trust of the God who is trustworthy could lead them to trust in God for better relations with one another. They learned to extend their trust of God and Jesus to other people. They risked being vulnerable with one another. Sure, there were flops and failures, including one leader in the church who chose to align with only one side of the discussion. His decision was subconscious, but still quite clear to those on the other side. This pastor was convinced the releases were right, and his view leaked out in the conversation at times, creating a lack of safety for some involved. Eventually, he ate some humble pie and confessed his views were not safe for all, and word spread that the pastor was coming around to being more trauma safe. Since safety creates trust, trust began to shift from the listening group to the other group, as well as from the other group to the listening group. And people in both camps began to trust that pastor as well. It took several months for this to happen, but it was clear to all involved that a new culture was forming in the church, a culture of expanded safety and trust.

We think Paul would be proud of this church's exploration of reconciliation.

We hope this deeper look at trauma, its effects, and how we respond has provided you with some new insights into the condition of the apostle Paul, a man far more vulnerable and in pain than many today recognize. By looking at how Paul handled his trauma in closer detail, we've gained a deeper understanding of how Paul's experience of trauma with the Corinthian church can, in turn, inform our experience today, leading to practices that Christian individuals and institutions can implement to create trauma-healthy spaces.

As we said when we started, a whole-body approach is needed for a community—and in particular a church—to become trauma healthy. The mind needs to be trauma informed, the ears need to become trauma sensitive, and the eyes need to look for what is trauma safe as the whole body yearns for spaces that are trauma healthy. May the Lord bless the body of Christ in its efforts to become trauma informed, trauma safe, and trauma healthy as we learn from the experience of Paul and the wisdom of God's Word, applying it to our lives today.

Acknowledgments

Scot

Kris and I thank Kelly and Karen for listening to my chatter about the subject of this book over the last two years. Their "I can't wait to read this book" has kept the project afloat. Kelly and Karen, named The Girls by Kris, have become close friends through thick and thin, through sharing their lives with us. Our lives are richer in love because of them. We dedicate this book to them. Thanks to Lisa Harper for providing a platform for me to present some of the ideas of this book at Kerygma 2025 in Nashville. And thanks to Rodney Reeves for reading and offering feedback on the Paul sections.

I can only mention that there were many others, including numerous podcasters, to whom Adrienne and I have talked about this book. I offer a special thanks to Adrienne, who in her thesis on trauma opened my eyes anew to how better to explain Paul when he gets so cranky. I want to thank Kris, who on our daily walks around the local lake hears what I'm writing about for the day and who offers her own wisdom about trauma. That wisdom is found often in this book.

Adrienne

Thank you, Matt, for believing in my capabilities. Sometimes attempting to do everything can be a large load to tackle. You encouraged me to take the time to sit down and write these words. But behind the scenes you loved our children, cleaned the house, and helped me manage my own counseling business. Starting Valor Counseling (www.valorcounselingaz.com) while writing a book was possible only because of you. Much love to the Gertie Girls (and boys)! We walked alongside each other for four years through seminary, and you all helped me dream this dream to reality. You saw something there before I even did. I will always think of our adventure in Greece and Turkey when I see this book. Scot, thank you for answering my question in the Chicago airport in 2022: Why did a trauma therapist get a master's in New Testament? You looked me straight in the eye and with all seriousness said, "So we can write a book together."

Notes

Chapter 1: Understanding Trauma: A Sketch

1. Judith Herman, *Trauma and Recovery* (New York: Basic Books, 1997), 33.
2. For an exceptional study of trauma studies, by an author who defines it similarly, see Pete Singer, "Toward a More Trauma-Informed Church: Equipping Faith Communities to Prevent and Respond to Abuse," *Currents in Theology and Mission* 51, no. 1 (January 2024): 62–76.
3. Substance Abuse and Mental Health Services Administration, *SAMHSA's Concept of Trauma and Guidance for a Trauma-Informed Approach*, HHS publication number (SMA) 14-4884 (Rockville, MD: Substance Abuse and Mental Health Services Administration, 2014), 7.
4. Peter Levine, *Healing Trauma: A Pioneering Program for Restoring the Wisdom of Your Body* (Boulder, CO: Sounds True, 2008), 8.
5. Bessel A. van der Kolk, *The Body Keeps the Score: Brain, Mind, and Body in the Healing of Trauma* (New York: Penguin, 2014), 21.
6. Nancy French (@NancyAFrench), "Today, I'm starting 'red devil' chemo," Twitter (now X), March 6, 2024, https://x.com/NancyAFrench/status/1765418095701852275.
7. Mayo Clinic Staff, "Dissociative Disorders," Mayo Clinic, August 31, 2023, www.mayoclinic.org/diseases-conditions/dissociative-disorders/symptoms-causes/syc-20355215. "The American Psychiatric Association defines three major dissociative disorders: Depersonalization/derealization disorder, dissociative amnesia, and dissociative identity disorder" (ibid).

Chapter 2: Trauma: More Than an Event

1. Substance Abuse and Mental Health Services Administration, *SAMHSA's Concept of Trauma and Guidance for a Trauma-Informed Approach,* HHS publication number (SMA) 14-4884 (Rockville, MD: Substance Abuse and Mental Health Services Administration, 2014), 7.
2. Bessel A. van der Kolk, *The Body Keeps the Score: Brain, Mind, and Body in the Healing of Trauma* (New York: Penguin, 2014), 43, 67, 177–79, 221.
3. Sandra Bloom, *Creating Sanctuary* (New York: Routledge, 2013), 37.
4. Peter Smith, "US Pastors Struggle with Post-Pandemic Burnout. Survey Shows Half Considered Quitting Since 2020," Associated Press, January 11, 2024, https://apnews.com/article/christian-clergy-burnout-pandemic-survey-24ee46327438ff46b074d234ffe2f58c. The study by the research project Exploring the Pandemic Impact on Congregations can be found at this link: chrome-extension://efaidnbmnnnibpcajpcglclefindmkaj/https://www.covidreligionresearch.org/wp-content/uploads/2024/01/Clergy_Discontentment_Patterns_Final.pdf. All details and quotations in this section come from these two sources.
5. Exploring the Pandemic Impact, 9–10.
6. Chip Rotolo et al., "Eight in Ten Americans Say Religion Is Losing Influence in Public Life," Pew Research Center, March 15, 2024, www.pewresearch.org/religion/2024/03/15/8-in-10-americans-say-religion-is-losing-influence-in-public-life/.
7. Exploring the Pandemic Impact, 12.
8. Exploring the Pandemic Impact, 22.
9. Exploring the Pandemic Impact, 23.
10. Scot McKnight and Laura Barringer, *A Church Called Tov: Forming a Goodness Culture That Resists Abuses of Power and Promotes Healing* (Carol Stream, IL: Tyndale Momentum, 2020); Scot McKnight and Laura Barringer, *Pivot: The Priorities, Practices, and Powers That Can Transform Your Church into a Tov Culture* (Carol Stream, IL: Tyndale Elevate, 2023).

Chapter 3: Trauma's Symptoms

1. Peter Yuichi Clark, "Toward a Pastoral Reading of 2 Corinthians as a Memoir of PTSD and Healing," in *Bible Through the Lens of Trauma*, ed. Elizabeth Boase and Christopher G. Frechette, Semeia Studies 86 (Atlanta: SBL Press, 2016), 232.
2. Lisa Oakley and Justin Humphreys, *Escaping the Maze of Spiritual Abuse: Creating Healthy Christian Cultures* (London: SPCK, 2019), 31.
3. Randal Rauser and Bob Stenhouse, *Disabuse: How to Prevent, Detect, Investigate, and Eliminate Abuse in Churches and Faith-Based Organizations* (Edmonton, Alberta: Veritas Solutions, 2025), 48.
4. Rauser and Stenhouse, *Disabuse*, 49.
5. Rauser and Stenhouse, *Disabuse*, 49–50, citing *Psychology Today*'s definition. See "Emotional Abuse," *Psychology Today*, www.psychologytoday.com/ca/basics/emotional-abuse.
6. Judith Herman, *Trauma and Recovery* (New York: Basic Books, 1997), 35.
7. Herman, *Trauma and Recovery*, 51.
8. Rauser and Stenhouse, *Disabuse*, 34–35.

Chapter 4: Listening to a Backstory

1. P. D. James, *Death in Holy Orders* (New York: Knopf, 2001), 94–95.
2. Michelle K. Keener, *Comfort in the Ashes: Explorations in the Book of Job to Support Trauma Survivors* (Downers Grove, IL: IVP Academic, 2025). Paynter's endorsement is found on the flyleaf of the book.
3. Laura van Dernoot Lipsky with Connie Burk, *Trauma Stewardship: An Everyday Guide to Caring for Self While Caring for Others* (San Francisco: Berrett-Koehler, 2009), 12.
4. This entire section is a rewrite of pages 6–12 of Scot McKnight, *1 Corinthians: Living Together in a Church Divided*, Everyday Bible Studies (Grand Rapids: HarperChristian Resources, 2024).
5. Ramani Durvasula, *It's Not You: Identifying and Healing from Narcissistic People* (New York: The Open Field/Penguin Life, 2024), 5–6.

6. For more on sealioning, which evokes the constant rising to a new surface of sea lions, see www.merriam-webster.com/wordplay /sealioning-internet-trolling.
7. On grandstanding, see Justin Tosi and Brandon Warmke, *Grandstanding: The Use and Abuse of Moral Talk* (New York: Oxford University Press, 2020).
8. Lil Copan, *Little Hours: A Novel* (Falmouth, MA: One Bird Books, 2021), 27.
9. These texts are from my *The Second Testament: A New Translation* (Downers Grove, IL: IVP Academic, 2023).
10. Murray J. Harris, *The Second Epistle to the Corinthians*, New International Greek Testament Commentary (Grand Rapids: Eerdmans, 2005); Ralph P. Martin, *2 Corinthians*, 2d ed., Word Biblical Commentary 40 (Grand Rapids: Zondervan, 2014). For a similar sketch of mine, see the introduction to *2 Corinthians: Leading in the Middle of Tension*, Everyday Bible Studies (Grand Rapids: HarperChristian Resources, 2024), 7–9.
11. Harris, *Second Epistle*, 101–5; Martin, *2 Corinthians*, 35–36. I have had this ever-adjusting sketch in my notes for years, which began in a 2 Corinthians class with Murray Harris in the spring of 1977, if my memory of the date is accurate.
12. Paul Barnett, *Paul: A Pastor's Heart in Second Corinthians* (Sydney South: Aquila Press, 2012), 55.
13. Barbara Brown Taylor, *Home by Another Way* (Lanham, MD: Rowman and Littlefield, 1999), 171.
14. Matthew Pawlak, "Consistency Isn't Everything: Self-Commendation in 2 Corinthians," *Journal for the Study of the New Testament* 40, no. 3 (2018): 360–82.

Chapter 5: Listening to Allegations

1. E. B. White, *Essays of E. B. White* (New York: Harper Perennial, 1999), 57.
2. Isaac T. Soon, *A Disabled Apostle: Impairment and Disability in the*

Letters of Paul (Oxford: Oxford University Press, 2023). The substance of this section depends on Soon's work.

3. Soon, *Disabled Apostle*, 175–76.
4. "Achondroplasia," Johns Hopkins Medicine, www.hopkinsmedicine.org/health/conditions-and-diseases/achondroplasia.
5. Soon, *Disabled Apostle*, 195.
6. Josephus, *Antiquities* 17.273, 278–79.
7. Jennifer Hrynyk, "What Should We Wear? The Clergy Clothing Quandry," April 20, 2021, Candler Doctor of Ministry Projects, https://scholarblogs.emory.edu/candlerdmin/2021/04/20/what-should-we-wear/.
8. Ralph P. Martin, *2 Corinthians*, 2d ed., Word Biblical Commentary 40 (Grand Rapids: Zondervan, 2014), 487.
9. Flavius Josephus, *Life of Josephus*, translation and commentary by Steve Mason (Leiden: Brill, 2003), 8–12.
10. Verlyn Verbrugge and Keith R. Krell, *Paul and Money: A Biblical and Theological Analysis of the Apostle's Teachings and Practices* (Grand Rapids: Zondervan, 2015).
11. For the image, Beverly R. Gaventa, *Our Mother Saint Paul* (Louisville: Westminster John Knox, 2007).
12. Andrew D. Clarke, *Secular and Christian Leadership in Corinth: A Socio-Historical and Exegetical Study of 1 Corinthians 1–6*, Paternoster Biblical Monographs (Milton Keynes, England: Paternoster, 2006), 59–107.
13. American Psychiatric Association, *Diagnostic and Statistical Manual of Mental Disorders, Text Revision*, 5th ed. (Washington, DC: American Psychiatric Publishing, 2022).
14. The following passages in 2 Corinthians informed Clark's diagnosis: 1:3–10; 4:7–12; 6:4–10; 11:21–33; 12:7–10.
15. Peter Yuichi Clark, "Toward a Pastoral Reading of 2 Corinthians as a Memoir of PTSD and Healing," in *Bible Through the Lens of Trauma*, ed. Elizabeth Boase and Christopher G. Frechette, Semeia Studies 86 (Atlanta: SBL Press, 2016), 234–41.

Chapter 6: Listening to Explanations 1

1. If you can't read Greek, my translation of 2 Corinthians 10–13 in *The Second Testament: A New Translation* can give you a feel for the jerkiness of his Greek.
2. *The Selected Letters of Willa Cather*, ed. Andrew Jewell and Janis Stout (New York: Vintage, 2014), 226.
3. *Selected Letters of Willa Cather*, 224.
4. For a wonderful exposition of the gospel of yes, see Mike Glenn, *The Gospel of Yes* (Colorado Springs: WaterBrook, 2012).
5. "Watch Male Pastors Read Sexist Comments Female Pastors Have Actually Been Told," *Relevant*, June 20, 2019, https://relevantmagazine.com/faith/watch-male-pastors-read-sexist-comments-female-pastors-have-actually-been-told/.
6. Cynthia Beach, *The Surface of Water: A Novel* (Downers Grove, IL: InterVarsity Press, 2024).
7. Steve Carter, *Grieve, Breathe, Receive: Finding a Faith Strong Enough to Hold Us* (Nashville: W Publishing, 2024), 34. These are listed in his text.
8. Carter, *Grieve, Breathe, Receive*, 67, 69. In his text much of the second paragraph is formatted into a list.

Chapter 7: Listening to Explanations 2

1. Kristin Du Mez, "Between Good and Evil: A Challenge for Christians in the Days Ahead," Du Mez Connections, January 23, 2025, https://kristindumez.substack.com/p/between-good-and-evil.
2. Dio Chrysostom, *To the People of Rhodes*, 16.
3. Leo Tolstoy, "The Story of Iván the Fool," in *Collected Shorter Fiction*, trans. Louise and Aylmer Maude and Nigel J. Cooper, vol. 2, Everyman's Library 243 (New York: Knopf, 2001), 65–93.
4. Ronald F. Hock, *The Social Context of Paul's Ministry: Tentmaking and Apostleship* (1980; Minneapolis: Fortress, 2007).
5. Carol Howard and James Fenimore, *Wounded Pastors: Navigating Burnout,*

Finding Healing, and Discerning the Future of Your Ministry (Louisville: Westminster John Knox, 2024), 107–10, quotes from 107, 110.

6. For a suggestive study on using labels for others, see Bruce J. Malina and Jerome H. Neyrey, *Calling Jesus Names: The Social Value of Labels in Matthew* (Sonoma, CA: Polebridge, 1988).

Chapter 8: Listening to Emotions

1. "Managing Anger—Yours and Others," Vancouver Island University, https://adm.viu.ca/workplace-conflict/managing-anger-yours-and-others.
2. Matthew Pawlak, *Sarcasm in Paul's Letters*, Society for New Testament Studies Monograph Series 182 (Cambridge: Cambridge University Press, 2023). "Both group sarcasm and irony together along with a constellation of related terms such as self-deprecating irony (*asteïsmos*), negation (*antiphrasis*), mockery (*myktērismos*), wit (*charientismos*), and derision (*epikertomēsis*). We may take this cluster of tropes as significant" (14). Note: I slightly reduced Pawlak's sentence. For another study, see Peter Yuichi Clark, "Toward a Pastoral Reading of 2 Corinthians as a Memoir of PTSD and Healing," in *Bible Through the Lens of Trauma*, ed. Elizabeth Boase and Christopher G. Frechette, Semeia Studies 86 (Atlanta: SBL Press, 2016).
3. Pawlak, *Sarcasm in Paul's Letters*, 1.
4. Pawlak, *Sarcasm in Paul's Letters*, 32.
5. Pawlak, *Sarcasm in Paul's Letters*, 211.
6. Pawlak, *Sarcasm in Paul's Letters*, 217.
7. Pawlak, *Sarcasm in Paul's Letters*, 218.
8. N. T. Wright, *Paul: A Biography* (San Francisco: HarperOne, 2018), 303.

Chapter 9: Safety

1. Brené Brown, *I Thought It Was Just Me (but It Isn't): Making the Journey from "What Will People Think?" to "I Am Enough"* (New York: Avery, 2007), 5.
2. Tricia Lott Williford, with Jana Richardson, *You Are Safe Now: A*

Survivor's Guide to Listening to Your Gut, Healing from Abuse, and Living in Freedom (Colorado Springs: NavPress, 2024), 95.

3. Diane Langberg, *Redeeming Power: Understanding Authority and Abuse in the Church* (Grand Rapids: Brazos, 2020), 25.

Chapter 10: Boundaries

1. Sandra L. Bloom, "Trauma Theory," in *Humanising Mental Health Care in Australia: A Guide to Trauma-Informed Approaches*, ed. Richard Benjamin, Joan Haliburn, and Serena King (New York: Routledge, 2019), 10.
2. A widely read study of boundaries is Henry Cloud and John Townsend, *Boundaries: When to Say Yes, How to Say No to Take Control of Your Life*, updated and expanded (Grand Rapids: Zondervan, 2017).
3. Nedra Glover Tawwab, *Set Boundaries, Find Peace: A Guide to Reclaiming Yourself* (New York: Tarcher, 2021), 5.
4. Cloud and Townsend, *Boundaries*, 107.
5. Aristotle, *Nicomachean Ethics* 8.3.1–6.

Chapter 12: Mutuality

1. Susan Grove Eastman, *Paul and the Person: Reframing Paul's Anthropology* (Grand Rapids: Eerdmans, 2017).
2. *The Roys Report*, https://julieroys.com.
3. Gabor Maté, *Scattered Minds: The Origins and Healing of Attention Deficit Disorder* (New York: Avery, 1999), 69–75.
4. Jenn Cusick, "SAMHSA's Six Principles of Trauma-Informed Care," in *Post-Secondary Peer Support Training Curriculum*, ed. Annie Brandner (BCCampus, 2022), https://opentextbc.ca/peersupport/chapter/samhsas-six-principles-of-trauma-informed-care.
5. Diane Langberg, *Redeeming Power: Understanding Authority and Abuse in the Church* (Grand Rapids: Brazos, 2020), 83.
6. Judith Herman, *Trauma and Recovery* (New York: Basic Books, 1997), 214.

Chapter 13: Empowerment

1. Judith Herman, *Trauma and Recovery* (New York: Basic Books, 1997), 133.
2. Herman, *Trauma and Recovery*, 8.
3. Scot McKnight and Laura Barringer, *A Church Called Tov: Forming a Goodness Culture That Resists Abuses of Power and Promotes Healing* (Carol Stream, IL: Tyndale Momentum, 2020), 41–53, 55–80.
4. Scott Giacomucci, *Trauma-Informed Principles in Group Therapy, Psychodrama, and Organizations: Action Methods for Leadership* (New York: Routledge, 2023), 211.
5. Childhelp, www.childhelp.org.
6. An excellent example of this can be found in Randal Rauser and Bob Stenhouse, *Disabuse: How to Prevent, Detect, Investigate, and Eliminate Abuse in Churches and Faith-Based Organizations* (Veritas Solutions, 2025). Stenhouse is an investigator, Rauser a theologian. Their book is a textbook on what to do.
7. Bruce D. Perry and Maia Szalavitz, *The Boy Who Was Raised as a Dog: And Other Stories from a Child Psychiatrist's Notebook* (2006; New York: Basic Books, 2017), 107–35.
8. Bessel A. van der Kolk, *The Body Keeps the Score: Brain, Mind, and Body in the Healing of Trauma* (New York: Penguin, 2014), 43–44.
9. Giacomucci, *Trauma-Informed Principles*, 211–12.

Chapter 14: Cultural Awareness

1. For a study that examines the percentage of women who tell the truth when they make allegations against church leaders, see Becky Castle Miller, "Living the King Jesus Gospel by Caring for Abuse Survivors," in *Living the King Jesus Gospel: Discipleship and Ministry Then and Now*, ed. Nijay K. Gupta et al. (Eugene, OR: Cascade, 2021), 235–48.
2. Pamela A. Hays, *Addressing Cultural Complexities in Practice: Assessment, Diagnosis and Therapy* (Washington DC: American Psychological Association, 2008), 3–18.
3. Korie L. Edwards, *The Elusive Dream: The Power of Race in Interracial*

Churches (New York: Oxford University Press, 2008); Korie Little Edwards and Rebecca Y. Kim, *Estranged Pioneers: Race, Faith, and Leadership in a Diverse World* (New York: Oxford University Press, 2024).

4. Derwin L. Gray, *Building a Multiethnic Church: A Gospel Vision of Love, Grace, and Reconciliation in a Divided World* (Nashville: Thomas Nelson, 2021).
5. Scott Giacomucci, *Trauma-Informed Principles in Group Therapy, Psychodrama, and Organizations: Action Methods for Leadership* (New York: Routledge, 2023), 230–32.

Chapter 15: Striving for Trauma-Healthy Spaces

1. Michael J. Gorman, *Cruciformity: Paul's Narrative Spirituality of the Cross*, new ed. (2001; Grand Rapids: Eerdmans, 2020); Michael J. Gorman, *Inhabiting the Cruciform God: Kenosis, Justification, and Theosis in Paul's Narrative Soteriology* (Grand Rapids: Eerdmans, 2009); Michael J. Gorman, *Becoming the Gospel: Paul, Participation, and Mission* (Grand Rapids: Eerdmans, 2015).
2. Scot McKnight, *Pastor Paul: Nurturing a Culture of Christoformity in the Church*, Theological Explorations for the Church Catholic (Grand Rapids: Brazos, 2019), 4–30.
3. Scot McKnight and Laura Barringer, *Pivot: The Priorities, Practices, and Powers That Can Transform Your Church into a Tov Culture* (Carol Stream, IL: Tyndale Elevate, 2023), 38.
4. Philip Plyming, *Being Real: The Apostle Paul's Hardship Narratives and the Stories We Tell Today* (London: SCM, 2023), 72–73.
5. I learned what I have quoted and summarized by SAMHSA from Pete Singer, "Toward a More Trauma-Informed Church: Equipping Faith Communities to Prevent and Respond to Abuse," *Currents in Theology and Mission* 51, no. 1 (January 2024): 62–76.
6. I reformatted their list. Substance Abuse and Mental Health Services Administration, *Trauma-Informed Care in Behavioral Health Services*, Treatment Improvement Protocol (TIP) Series 57, HHS Publication No. (SMA) 13-4801 (Rockville, MD: Substance Abuse and Mental

Health Services Administration, 2014), www.ncbi.nlm.nih.gov/books /NBK207201.

7. Teresa Morgan, *Trust in Atonement: God, Creation, and Reconciliation* (Grand Rapids: Eerdmans, 2024), 89–90.
8. Morgan, *Trust in Atonement*, 114.

Revelation for the Rest of Us

A Prophetic Call to Follow Jesus as a Dissident Disciple

Scot McKnight with Cody Matchett

ISBN: 9780310179009

See how the Book of Revelation can be read as a book of discipleship, challenging Christ-followers everywhere to live as hopeful agents of resistance and transformation.

The final book of the Bible frustrates and frightens many people with its imagery and apocalyptic tone. Popular interpretations rely on fear and politicization and often lead to pride and alienation of others. Is this really how we were intended to read John's Revelation?

In *Revelation for the Rest of Us*, Scot McKnight, with Cody Matchett, explores the key message of Revelation and how it:

- Calls us to be faithful and hopeful witnesses to Jesus.
- Stimulates our imagination to see the world through the eyes of God and excite our faith.
- Challenges us to stand against the militarism, economic exploitation, oppression, and injustice of worldly authorities.

McKnight addresses the popular misconceptions about the book, explaining what John means in his use of the images of dragons, lambs, and beasts; and how the symbolism of Revelation spoke in the days of Rome and still speaks powerfully to the present day—though not in the way most people think.

You'll learn to see the Book of Revelation in a fresh and hopeful new way. Drawing from the latest scholarship, the authors present an understanding of Revelation for anyone interested in deepening their study of the Bible and strengthening their faith as dissident disciples who can discern the presence of "Babylon" in our world and learn to speak up, speak out, and walk in the way of the Lamb.

Invisible Jesus

A Book about Leaving the Church and Looking for Christ

Scot McKnight with Tommy Preson Phillips

ISBN: 9780310162315

Is deconstruction a rebellion against God or a prophetic movement resisting a distorted gospel?

In recent years, we've seen an increase in the number of Christians who are "deconstructing" their faith—critically analyzing Christianity and the church and finding that it falls short. Many end up leaving behind the beliefs and commitments they formerly held. While many have written on how to reverse this trend, Scot McKnight and Tommy Preson Phillips believe that deconstruction isn't a problem but a voice. And we need to listen to what it is saying to the church.

Deconstructors are uncovering serious weaknesses in today's church—a renewed fundamentalism, toxic leadership, and legalistic thinking among them. Using the results of recent studies by Pew, Gallup, and others, McKnight and Phillips take a careful look at what deconstructors are really saying, seeking to better understand why many are shedding elements of the faith and church of their youth but also engaging in a reconstruction process, finding Jesus afresh. They are losing their religion but not losing Jesus.

Filled with stories of those who have walked the path of deconstruction without losing their faith, *Invisible Jesus* is a prophetic call to examine ourselves and discern whether the faith we practice and the church we belong to are really representative of the Jesus we follow. Each chapter looks at a different topic and offers biblical reflections that call for us not only to better listen but also to change how we live out our faith as Jesus' followers today.

2 Corinthians

Leading in the Middle of Tension

NEW TESTAMENT EVERYDAY
BIBLE STUDY SERIES

Scot McKnight

ISBN: 9780310129455

Scholarly Insights with a Pastoral Heart for All the Books of the New Testament

"Scot McKnight is one of my absolute favorite New Testament scholars, and his Everyday Bible Study series is akin to Einstein creating a user-friendly version of the theory of relativity!"
—Lisa Harper, award-winning author and Bible teacher

The apostle Paul's second letter to the Corinthians is Paul's most pastoral letter, his most emotional letter, and a view into the factions and the fracturing relations with one of his most memorable churches. In the letter, Paul appeals to unity and expresses joy over the good news he hears about Corinthian believers' reception of his care for them.

In the New Testament Everyday Bible Study Series, widely respected biblical scholar Scot McKnight reveals the newness and activeness of God's Word as it works in our everyday lives. His unique approach to Bible study combines sound theology with relevant pastoral wisdom. Each volume of this series provides the following:

- *Original Meaning:* brief, precise expositions of the biblical text and a clear focus for the central message of each passage.
- *Fresh Interpretation:* brings the passage alive with fresh images and what it means to follow King Jesus.
- *Practical Application:* biblical connections and questions for reflection and application for each passage.

McKnight uses the NIV as the primary Bible text, but he also includes insights from his own translation of the entire New Testament. Each Bible study features a short, compact, clear exposition that both summarizes the whole and gives the reader a clear focus for what is central to the passage.

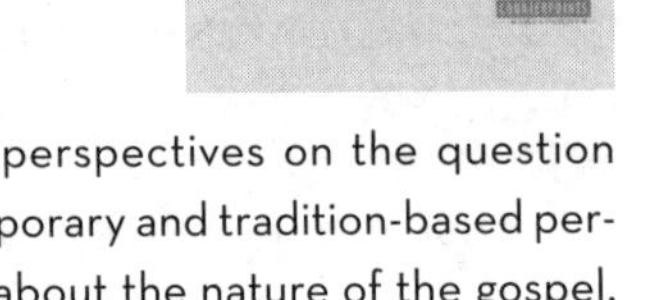

Five Views on the Gospel

Counterpoints: Bible and Theology

Michael Horton, Scot McKnight, David A. deSilva, Julie C. Ma, Shively T. J. Smith, contributors

Michael F. Bird and Jason S. Maston, editors

ISBN: 9780310128533

Five Views on the Gospel presents five different perspectives on the question "What is the gospel?" Presenting a variety of contemporary and tradition-based perspectives, each contributor answers key questions about the nature of the gospel. Questions include:

- What is the gospel?
- What is the context for understanding the New Testament teaching about the gospel?
- What are the primary biblical texts that you believe express the gospel and how do you understand them?
- What are people called to do with the gospel and what are the benefits promised by the gospel?
- How can the definition and proclamation of the gospel be contextualized and made relevant today?
- What example of an inadequate gospel and a false gospel can you offer?
- What does it mean to live a life worthy of the gospel?

The Counterpoints format provides a unique opportunity for each contributor to set forth their own understanding of the gospel and to interact with competing perspectives, and for the editors to sum up points of agreement and disagreement and a path forward in the debate.

Positions and contributors include:

- The Reformation Gospel (Michael Horton)
- The King Jesus Gospel (Scot McKnight)
- The Wesleyan Gospel (David A. deSilva)
- The Pentecostal Gospel (Julie C. Ma)
- A Liberation Theology Gospel (Shively T. J. Smith)

The Counterpoints series presents a comparison and critique of scholarly views on topics important to Christians that are both fair-minded and respectful of the biblical text. Each volume is a one-stop reference that allows readers to evaluate the different positions on a specific issue and form their own, educated opinion.